ADULTS' GUIDE TO
SWIMMING
It's never too late to learn

BY
PETRINA LIYANAGE

ADULTS' GUIDE TO SWIMMING
It's never too late to learn
Copyright © 2020 Petrina Liyanage

Illustrations by Tanya Leontyeva
Cover photography by Jolene Holten
Cover design by Hammad Khalid
Videos by Tomas Cottenie

Published by Change Empire Books
https://www.changeempire.com

ISBN: 978-0-6487453-3-4

"Petrina is an excellent swim training specialist for adults."
Alan Joyce AC
Managing Director and Chief Executive Officer, Qantas Airways Limited

"Petrina is an amazing swim coach. Learning to swim has been an empowering experience for me. Now at the age of fifty-five, I can swim with confidence."
Sudhir Warrier
Chairman, Australian Cruise Group

TABLE OF CONTENTS

ACKNOWLEDGEMENTS

First and foremost, sincere thanks to **my students** who've taught me so much. Without their trust and openness, I would never have been able to build upon the insight and knowledge over the years to continually improve my specialised service.

AUSTSWIM (Australia's leading organisation for the training of teachers of swimming and water safety) whose public recognition of my work, through state and national industry awards of excellence in 2018, has been pivotal in empowering me to write this book and promote the ongoing need for adult education in swimming and survival skills. I would like to thank in particular **Craig Halliday** and **Robyn Larkham** for their feedback to help shape this book.

Dr Alan Pearce (Associate Professor, Neurophysiologist, Australia) who generously dedicated his time to explain the science behind the theory of neuroplasticity and help to reinforce my message that learning a new skill later in life is most certainly achievable.

Dr Steven N Blair (Distinguished Professor Emeritus, Exercise Scientist, U.S.A.) whose comprehensive lifestyle study over thirty-two years raised the profile internationally of the multiple health benefits of swimming compared with other physical activities.

Kaye Wood (Royal Life Saving Society, New South Wales, Australia) who very promptly assisted with many ad hoc requests for information and guidance during the compilation of this book.

Joanna Milburn and **Dr Gillian Spalding-Stracey** who both kindly volunteered their editorial expertise with my manuscript.

Pia Saithanu who graciously agreed to be photographed for the front cover of this book.

Tomas Cottenie without whose love and encouragement this book might never have been written.

PREFACE

I've deliberately crafted the wording and exercises in this book to be relevant for the everyday person who wishes to become confident and broadly competent in the water, rather than to qualify for the Olympics!

If you follow the **step-by-step instructions**, you'll embark upon an exciting journey towards doubling your world by discovering the thrill of being in water in addition to life on land.

Although I cannot offer any guarantees of success, this book collates my proven teaching methods which have effectively helped many to master their desired aquatic skills.

My intention is to teach you the fundamental skills in order to swim and survive. I've not delved into the more technical details such as the exact degree that your hands should be angled when doing a stroke, or the precise number of centimetres your feet should be from the surface when kicking. My instructions are of a *general* nature; to empower you with the confidence to feel comfortable in the water and in control of it.

Wherever possible **I've explained the reason behind common problems** that adults encounter, which my students tell me is often neglected by some swim schools. If you can't identify technical faults and understand why they're wrong, you can develop bad habits that are inefficient and this can lead to frustration.

Please refer to the glossary at the back of this book for any terminology that may be new to you.

I hope you enjoy reading this book as much as I've enjoyed writing it. The guidance I regularly give to my students on their personal swimming journey has in fact proved very pertinent to me on my own writing journey.

- There are most certainly others going through the same challenges as yourself, asking the same questions as you and sharing the same insecurities. You may feel like you're the only one, but **you're not alone.**

- Taking the decision to go for it may seem daunting, particularly if you've been trying to ignore that inner voice inside, nagging you to do it for a long while. It can **challenge your self-belief.**

- I started with a blank page in Microsoft Word, similar to swim students who say, "Teach me from scratch". It may be difficult to stay focused and motivated. **Be patient, take baby steps and always reflect upon how far you've come**. You'll soon be feeling accomplished as you upskill.

- Both swimming and writing need to be built into your routine in order to see results. I've been guilty of letting days and weeks slip by, which has proven detrimental to publishing this book sooner. (In fact, completing this book has taken far longer than teaching any adult to learn to swim.) **Discipline is absolutely crucial** to maintain momentum.

- The success in achieving your goal is ultimately down to you. It doesn't mean though that you should pursue your efforts alone. **Sharing your journey** with close family and friends can be an invaluable source of support.

DISCLAIMER

This book is for your guidance and support i.e. for educational purposes only. I hope it empowers you with the confidence to perform vital swimming and water safety skills, as it's intended.

Please note that I cannot accept any responsibility or liability for any injury or loss sustained as a result of using or in connection with this material to help yourself or others.

WATER SAFETY

A big part of building your confidence will be about being safe in the water so that you can relax and learn productively and positively.

It's *your* responsibility to ensure your own water safety, with due consideration given to the following factors.

- Your current level of ability.

- Your current level of fitness.

- Your current level of fear (if relevant). If you feel very anxious or too nervous to carry out the suggested exercises in the water by yourself, take someone along with you who is calm, patient, supportive and a good swimmer.

- Your current overall health. If you're feeling unwell then it's not recommended to enter the water. That includes the common cold, which can make breathing difficult.

- Any medications which may affect your mobility or mindset.

- Any medical conditions such as (but not limited to):
    - Arthritis
    - Asthma
    - Diabetes
    - Coronary heart disease
    - Epilepsy
    - High blood pressure
    - Stroke
    - Joint problems
    - Previous injuries
    - Being prone to ear or eye infections
    - Pregnancy

If you have any concerns about undertaking activities in the water, it's *your* responsibility to seek medical advice/clearance before proceeding.

The exercises in this book are described with the 'general' adult body in mind i.e. without any specific restrictions in physical ability. Please ensure that you adapt the prescribed activity to work around any physical limitations you may have, in order to minimise the risk of any adverse outcome.

EXERTION

How you choose to use this book is at your own discretion. We as individuals all have our own various physical and psychological attributes, which means that the same exercise will require a different intensity of effort from person-to-person based on factors such as age and health (both in body and mind).

Wherever possible, I've suggested easier alternatives if you find a certain exercise too challenging, for example by using a flotation aid or simply walking the exercise.

It's important to work at your own pace, but to keep challenging yourself in order to continue progressing forward, rather than 'feeling content' at a certain level (unless that's the only level you wish to reach, of course). This doesn't mean though that you should push yourself unreasonably beyond your own capabilities.

If you experience any signs of overexertion such as (but not limited to):

- Severe breathlessness
- Dizziness
- Nausea
- Pain or tightness in the chest

Then you should stop your practice session immediately and seek medical advice.

ICONS USED IN THIS BOOK

VIDEO

An online demonstration video is available at
bit.ly/adultsguidetoswimmingvideos

HOME

A land exercise to practise at home.

EXERCISE

A water exercise to practise in the pool.

TIPS

An alternative description or suggestion to help you to understand or perform the exercise more easily.

NOTES

A description of what you might be experiencing or questioning, and the answer behind it.

ALERT

A point to be wary of.

KICKBOARD

A kickboard is recommended to use for this exercise.

NOODLE

A noodle is recommended to use for this exercise.

PULLBUOY

A pullbuoy is recommended to use for this exercise.

SNORKEL

A snorkel is recommended to use for this exercise.

FINS

A pair of short blade fins is recommended to use for this exercise.

CHAPTERS

📽 ✇ Ex 14I: Freestyle using one side of body
📽 ✇ Ex 14J: Flutter kicking and stroking independently
📽 ✇ Ex 14K: Complete freestyle

15 ADVANCED SKILLS

15.1 Linking laps between strokes

📽 ✇ Ex 15A: Front torpedo ('push and glide')
📽 ✇ Ex 15B: Back torpedo ('push and glide')
📽 ✇ Ex 15C: From a front stroke to a front stroke: touch turn
📽 ✇ Ex 15D: From a front stroke to a back stroke: turn
📽 ✇ Ex 15E: From a back stroke to a front stroke: turn
📽 ✇ Ex 15F: From a back stroke to a back stroke: turn

15.2 Linking between treading water and a stroke

✇ Ex 15G: From treading water to a front stroke
✇ Ex 15H: From treading water to a back stroke
✇ Ex 15I: From a front or back stroke to treading water

15.3 Confidence in deep water

✇ Ex 15J: Resurfacing after submerging into deep water
📽 ✇ Ex 15K: Snorkelling
✇ Ex 15L: Swimming over deep water
📽 ✇ Ex 15M: Swimming underwater

15.4 Swimming in open water

1: ME & THIS BOOK

1.1 ABOUT ME

My parents originate from Sri Lanka and Malaysia and have never been confident swimmers themselves. In fact, they took adult beginner lessons before they had my sister and I. Although they ensured I had lessons as a child, I only rediscovered the joy of swimming in my early twenties and decided to share my passion for it by teaching it full-time from my early thirties. I never swam at a competitive level (unless you count racing my nephew).

So **I in fact refreshed my aquatic skills as an adult.** Through industry training to gain various swim teaching qualifications in Australia, I discovered that some techniques I learnt as a child are no longer considered correct. You may be surprised to learn that swimming theories and practices continue to evolve through ongoing research, even though the general principles remain the same.

I first gained teaching experience leading adult group classes at various swim schools across Sydney, before setting up my **own business running individual adult classes** in completely private pools, which for me has been both the most eye-opening and the most rewarding.

Through one-on-one tuition, I've had the privilege of getting to know my students pretty well. They've taught me so much more about learning to swim as an adult than any textbook has, and for that I'm forever grateful. I'll share plenty of real-life stories throughout this book, with names changed to maintain confidentiality.

1.2 THE TWO REASONS BEHIND WRITING THIS BOOK

- **To help people discover the enjoyment of being in water** as much as I do, whether you classify yourself as a complete beginner or someone who wishes to improve your existing skill set.

- **To break down what I believe is a social stigma surrounding the lack of aquatic skills that an adult can have.** In a country like Australia, swimming can arguably be perceived as a basic life skill like reading and writing, that you're presumed to have acquired from a very young age. People are often surprised to hear that I'm able to run a full-time business specialised in empowering adults with water confidence. Is there really a strong enough demand for such a service? The answer is a resounding yes, absolutely!

Between 1st July 2018 and 30th June 2019, adults (aged 18 and over) in Australia accounted for almost *seven times* the number of drowning deaths compared with that of children. Recreational swimming was the leading activity immediately prior to drowning[1].

The facts speak for themselves.

Interestingly, out of a total of 276 deaths of adults and children over this period, *just 16 were overseas tourists*[2].

Could that imply that Australian residents are more complacent or perhaps misguided about their water competency compared with overseas visitors who could be more acutely aware of their lack of aquatic skills? The jury's out on that one.

There's a heavy emphasis (and rightly so) on educating children in Australia on water safety from a very young age. But what about us grown-ups who seek this education too?

The lack of recognition of this need by adults has led to people seeking private individual lessons with a professional like myself because they feel too embarrassed to ask family or friends to teach them, and too intimidated to join a group class. A student Kate was in her mid-fifties when I met her, and always strategically booked beachside family holidays over winter to validate her excuse of never entering the water. (She also told me that she knew her kids suspected her inadequacies, but it was never spoken about.) This story is not uncommon for me to hear.

From my teaching experience I've come to recognise and appreciate the very strong psychological aspect to getting water confident as an adult. Every person I've had the fortune of helping has demonstrated a strong sense of determination, positivity and humility – that you most likely have too.

So, in addition to the practical exercises covered, this book also focuses on the importance of self-belief and ways to develop the right mindset to achieve success.

This book can be used to either support lessons you are or will be undertaking, or as a stand-alone aid to self-teach.

I hope you enjoy the read.

2: YOU & THIS BOOK

This book covers the beginning-to-end process behind getting water confident in a fairly simplified manner – it's not a highly technical guide and isn't written to benefit competition swimmers. It's broken down into a series of logical progressions, guiding you through the complete journey from getting prepared to enter the water, to building your skills in shallow and then deep water.

To be completely honest the best way to learn is face-to-face with a qualified swim teacher.

This book (and accompanying videos) provide great tools to self-teach if:

- You can't or don't wish to take swimming lessons.

- You wish to prepare yourself prior to taking swimming lessons.

- You seek to enhance your knowledge to complement current swimming lessons.

Some of you may want to learn everything, others may choose to refer to only certain chapters depending on your specific goals. Everybody's definition of water confidence will differ. Perhaps you'd like to be able to swim one stroke to do laps at a pool. Perhaps you'd like the confidence to jump in and tread water in the event you need to rescue your child. Or perhaps you simply wish to get comfortable at getting your face wet and move around so you can enjoy the water on holiday with a lifejacket on.

Whichever level you wish to reach, **I strongly encourage you to follow my progressions.** Just like learning any life skill such as driving, it's imperative to work through a logical series of steps in order of increasing complexity. The sequences I've detailed have proved an effective method to develop confidence and competence in the water, so please trust in the process.

If you can identify yourself with any of the following circumstances and motivations listed below, this book has been written for you.

2.1 YOUR CIRCUMSTANCES

- **You had the opportunity to learn at school,** but either had a poor teaching or learning experience, or have forgotten the skills and since lost confidence in the water.

- **Swimming was not a part of your culture** during childhood. You didn't have the access, opportunity or feel the necessity to learn. Your lack of exposure to water has led to you having little or no swimming experience as an adult.

- **You didn't have the financial means** to learn when younger.

- **You've a physical disability** which mentally prevented you from trying to learn earlier in life.

- **You suffered a water related trauma** and developed a fear or phobia. Many students in this situation remember their experience very vividly. Interestingly, a student Maria who was a confident swimmer throughout adulthood, recalled a drowning incident as a child whilst under hypnosis. This actually led to her developing a new fear of the water as an adult.

- **You've had a fear instilled in you** by others. A student Anna had a sister who died from drowning when they were swimming together as kids; and since then her parents had always forbidden her from ever going near the water.

- **Your parents were non-swimmers or poor swimmers,** and so never let you near the water. I've taught students who are driven to learn in order to avoid repeating this same situation with their own children.

- **You or someone close to you (not a teaching professional) taught you how to swim** and you wish to evaluate and improve your current techniques.

2.2 YOUR MOTIVATIONS

- You've had it **on your bucket list** to improve your current aquatic skills as you've long doubted whether you've been swimming correctly.

- You're embracing a new way of life and are excited by **the challenge of mastering a new life skill.** I've helped many people who've taken up swimming alongside other activities like learning to drive or learning a foreign language. Some have even decided to undertake a triathlon as a long-term goal.

- **You have (or are expecting to have) children or grandchildren** and want to be able to swim with them/rescue them in an emergency. A student Alice was triggered to learn during her divorce, as she'd always relied on her husband to take their kids swimming. A student Theo believed his son was starting to surpass his own capabilities and felt compelled to upskill. I've helped many students who are parents and invested the time and money into ensuring their children were water safe but had neglected themselves.

- **A medical professional recommended** you to take up swimming for rehabilitation, to ease ongoing problems (e.g. in the spine) or to boost mental health. A student Jessica suffered from chronic depression and discovered that swimming greatly helped to alleviate her symptoms.

- You wish to **improve your respiratory health** through aerobic exercise. A student Roy was an asthmatic sufferer. A student Alan was a professional opera singer and sought to improve his lung capacity for his performance on stage.

- You've an **injury or mobility restriction** that means you're now seeking alternative ways of exercise. This is a particularly popular reason for runners who have damaged knees and are looking for a low impact way to stay fit. The water's buoyancy means much less stress on joints and muscles allowing for a safer way to exercise through what is, in effect, resistance training.

- You're planning to **change careers** and need to undertake a swimming test in order to join a different profession (e.g. the police force, navy, airline, etc).

- You'd love to ultimately take part in an aquatic activity like surfing, kayaking or water-skiing. A student Jill planned to go **scuba diving** at the Great Barrier Reef and needed to undertake a swimming test as part of the assessment to gain the licence. A student Phil was in fact an Olympic rower but had never learnt how to tread water.

- You'd like to **adopt a more active lifestyle.** A study carried out over thirty-two years at the University of South Carolina U.S.A. revealed that amongst forty thousand men (aged twenty to ninety), swimmers had a fifty percent lower mortality rate than their sedentary peers or those who walked or ran[3].

- You'd like to embrace a **different way to exercise.** Swimming will never make you feel sweaty as the water around you constantly cools you down.

- You'd like **to lose weight or maintain weight control.** Swimming is a fantastic fat-burning workout, engaging all the major muscle groups for all-over body toning. A student Ross was previously an obese man in his thirties who sought a way to maintain his new body weight after losing a whopping fifty-three kilos! The water's resistance being twelve to fifteen times that of air allows for a very effective way to train[4].

- You're about to go on **holiday** (or have recently returned from one) and discovered you lack the water confidence to make the most of it. You're sick of missing out on opportunities and sitting next to the water, watching everyone else enjoy being in it.

- You're **retired or pregnant** and seeking a way to exercise which is low impact on the skeletal system and improves flexibility, balance, posture and circulation. Swimming works out all your body's major muscle systems in a safer way compared to land-based exercise, as it doesn't put strain on weight bearing joints.

2.3 OVERCOMING OBJECTIONS

- **It's never too late.** It really is possible – regardless of your age. My oldest complete beginner student was in her eighties. She had a backyard pool but never had the skills before to enjoy it. She sought the basic water confidence to know how to save herself in case she ever fell in whilst skimming the leaves from the surface – and to be able to finally enjoy swimming with her nine grandkids!

- **You don't need to be completely mobile and flexible.** It's a matter of identifying the way to move in the water that works for your body and is adapted to address any physical limitations you may have. A student Andrew had significant hip, back and shoulder restrictions. He knew he wouldn't be able to master the 'typical' way to swim *any* of the strokes. I developed a way for him to move his arms and legs in the water in order to get from A to B safely without his physical attributes limiting him. He can now swim laps at the pool to keep fit and enjoy the water. If you're concerned about any physical or medical issues you have, be sure to get medical clearance first from your doctor or healthcare professional.

- **You don't need to have an athletic body.** In fact, people with more body fat have better buoyancy – which is one of life's ironies. A student Anna always struggled with treading water as a skinny child but finds she can now do it with very minimal effort as a bigger sized adult. Don't forget that once you're in the water, nobody can see your body. Refer to Chapter 6.6 'Swimwear' for advice if you're body conscious.

- **You don't need to be able to float well.** From my experience, it's very rare to see an adult float for a long period of time. This is because as an adult, you've developed muscles in your legs that increase your density in the water. Children have less developed muscles, with their lungs contributing to a greater percentage of their total body mass. These combined factors mean they float easier and for longer. Women generally float a little better than men do, as their higher percentage of body fat improves buoyancy.

There are other factors that influence how long and how well you can float for which I'll cover in Chapter 10 'Floating horizontally'. Suffice to say here that as an adult, it's completely normal to not be able to float for a long period of time.

- **You're less likely to get injured** compared with land-based sports. In neck-deep water, a person weighs only around ten percent of what he or she does on land[5]; meaning you can work out more intensively without causing wear and tear on your joints or muscles. Having the water support most of your body weight can be particularly advantageous if you're pregnant, obese, or suffer from back pain or arthritis.

- **It doesn't matter how long it has been since the last time you were in the water.** A student Jessica hadn't dipped a toe in the water for over six decades. The most important thing is your motivation and personal commitment to succeed.

- The **weather doesn't need to be hot** in order to learn. There are plenty of indoor heated pools still operating over the cooler months.

- **The pool isn't always crowded and noisy.** Refer to Chapter 6.2 'Factors to consider when choosing a swimming pool' on how to find the right pool and the right time to visit.

- **You'll need to make the time.** Developing any new skill will naturally require a commitment of your time, regardless of how busy life gets. In the early stages of learning there may be some land exercises that can serve as the next best alternative if you struggle with getting to a pool for whatever reason. I've flagged these with the home icon (refer to 'Icons Used In This Book'). As you get more advanced, the only effective way to practise will be in the water.

- **It doesn't matter how many times you've tried before.** The human body and mind are only limited by the barriers we put upon ourselves. A student Pete undertook nine attempts before he took lessons with me and successfully achieved his goals. It's about finding the right teaching model that works for you.

2.4 YOU CAN DO IT: THE THEORY OF NEUROPLASTICITY

When I receive calls of enquiry from prospective students, I often sense the same apprehension about taking that step to learn. Some, like a student Greg, have wrestled internally with the decision over several decades.

The good news is that your adult brain is still responsive to sensory inputs, and new stimulation is great for brain health by keeping it responding and adapting through learning a new skill.

The theory of neuroplasticity – **the ability of the brain to reorganise and adapt continuously throughout an individual's life** – involves five key factors to success:

1. Task-dependent experience: being open to absorb new information and apply it to exercises.

2. Repetition and practice (I can't emphasise this enough!)

3. Self-motivation.

4. Quality of repetition: setting yourself goals to maintain focused.

5. Recognising the rewards: qualitatively (e.g. not swallowing water) and quantitatively (e.g. swimming a certain distance).

I married a Belgian and am currently learning his native language as well as learning how to play the drums as a hobby. I have no aspirations to become a translator or to join a rock band, just like you don't have aspirations to join the Olympics.

Developing new skills as an adult can challenge you – but it's also enjoyable and will ultimately provide a great sense of accomplishment, particularly if this has been on your bucket list for years.

2.5 SWIM LEARNER TYPES

From my experience, the definition of an adult swim learner is incredibly subjective! I've identified three broad categories of swimmers, which I'll be referring to throughout this book.

SWIM LEARNER TYPES

CURRENT COMFORTABLE DEPTH IN WATER	CAN GET FACE WET	SWIMMER TYPE
Ankle/knee deep.	No.	**SWIMMER A:** Beginner with fear of water.
Chest/neck deep.	Yes or no.	**SWIMMER B:** Beginner without fear of water.
Neck deep or out of depth.	Yes.	**SWIMMER C:** Swimmer that lacks technique.

2.6 HOW LONG WILL IT TAKE?

This is by far the most common question I get asked! How long is a piece of string? It will naturally depend on the level you start at, your level of fear (if any), your energy/focus levels, the frequency of your practice and your goals.

A student Jim needed ten one-hour sessions to focus solely on mastering an independent front float. This was due to a previous trauma in the water as a young child when his dad didn't follow through with his promise to catch him at the end of a water slide.

Conversely, I taught a student Nadine from scratch how to swim freestyle reasonably well in just seven thirty-minute sessions.

The bottom line is that it's important to be realistic and patient with yourself. A student Donna had to undergo a professional swimming test in order to join an airline as a stewardess. She had to be able to swim a certain distance and tread water for a certain amount of time. Despite being a complete beginner she rather ambitiously presumed she could learn all the skills competently over just four days. Needless to say she had to postpone her test.

Learning to swim is both physically *and* mentally tiring. You can keep your practice sessions short (say thirty minutes) – just ensure that you don't risk long gaps between sessions – you can otherwise lose momentum in both learning and confidence building.

Making time in your diary to get in the water on a regular basis will be important. You'll need to make it by building it into your busy routine. The below is an indication of the minimum frequency I'd recommend for practice. (If you can find the time to get in more often, all the better.)

Recommended frequency of practice

SWIMMER TYPE	FREQUENCY
SWIMMER A (BEGINNER WITH FEAR)	Ideally daily. The more basic a level you start at, the more frequently you should practise (at least at the beginning). You'll otherwise spend more time recapping exercises than progressing to the next level, and progress might be slow.
SWIMMER B (BEGINNER WITHOUT FEAR)	Twice weekly. You won't need to familiarise yourself with the basics of being in water and can proceed with exercises straight away.
SWIMMER C (THAT LACKS TECHNIQUE)	Once weekly. Your focus being to maintain the momentum of unlearning bad habits and reinforcing (new) correct skills through repetition.

3: TEN GOLDEN RULES TO GET WATER CONFIDENT

1. **Never underestimate the importance of relaxing.** It helps you to float and breathe better, which ultimately helps you to swim better.

2. **Never hold your breath;** always breathe in and out.

3. **Breathe in** *before* **your lungs are empty.** Don't wait until you've expelled all air, as this leads to gasping, panic and an erratic breathing pattern.

4. **The correct breath control is to inhale through mouth, and exhale through mouth and nose together.**

5. **Your head impacts your body position.** For example raising your head when horizontal causes your hips and legs to fall.

6. **Goggles are crucial** to expedite your water confidence when learning. It's important to keep your eyes open at all times. (You can transition away from wearing them later if you wish.)

7. Your **hands should be slightly cupped** for all movements in water. (Placing your hand on your thigh demonstrates the same curved shape.) **Fingers should be close together**, with **firm (not floppy) wrists.** The positioning of your feet and ankles will vary depending on the kick used.

8. **Always check the water depth** before entering. If you're anxious or nervous, **take a buddy with you** who's a good swimmer.

9. Learning how to tread **water is more tiring than people think. Practise in short bursts** to conserve energy and avoid frustration. You can focus on extending your time later once the technique is mastered.

10. **Be patient with yourself.** Mastering aquatic skills may take longer than you think, even if you consider yourself to be a fit person.

4: THREE STAGES IN THE LEARNING JOURNEY

1. Building confidence with the **basics**

2. Refining **technique**

3. Increasing **stamina**

This book predominantly focuses on the first and second stages. The third stage is explored in Chapter 15 'Advanced skills'.

NOTES

If you master a skill once, ensure you repeat it several times to reinforce it before moving on. A skill can easily be forgotten if not repeated. Be sure to embed the skill into your long-term memory by repeating it and consistently performing it well. This will also make you feel good!

5: GETTING READY: MINDSET

5.1 The types of fear that a swimmer can face
5.2 Conquering your fears
5.3 Ten tips to help you to prepare for the journey ahead

You may be feeling a little anxious about your journey to getting water confident. This is completely normal, particularly if you classify yourself as Swimmer A (beginner with fear).

5.1 THE TYPES OF FEAR THAT A SWIMMER CAN FACE

- **The fear of running out of air.**

This is about understanding your own lung capacity and developing the skill of anticipating the need to inhale, *before* your lungs are empty. If you wait too long and you do run out of air, you're likely to panic and gasp, which will break your confidence as well as your rhythm in the water.

Your lung capacity will be different if you're significantly unfit, a smoker, pregnant, or suffer any respiratory conditions like asthma.

NOTES

Refer to Chapter 9.3 'Breath control'.

TIPS

- **The fear of getting water in the nose and/or mouth.**

Technically, the correct way to exhale underwater is through both mouth and nose *together*. Expelling air from both channels should stop any water from entering.

However, it can be challenging for some to master this technique. The good news is that there are alternative ways.

Refer to Chapter 9.3 'Breath control' and Chapter 6.7 'Equipment to wear' for information on nose clips.

TIPS

- **The fear of getting water in the eyes.**

I strongly recommend investing in a pair of goggles to protect your eyes and enhance your confidence through clearer vision underwater.

Refer to Chapter 6.7 'Equipment to wear' for information on goggles.

TIPS

- **The fear of getting water in the ears.**

Your ears should submerge if you're horizontal in the water. Water that enters the ears will eventually flow back out. A student Fiona always recalled a traumatic memory of drowning whenever her ears were wet. If you can't get used to water in the ears, or are susceptible to ear infections, there are solutions available.

Refer to Chapter 6.7 'Equipment to wear' for information on ear plugs and caps that seal the ears.

TIPS

- **The fear of not being able to touch the ground with your feet, or the poolside with your hands.**

This is about developing a trust in the water to support you, and the ability to control your balance; most crucially how to stand up independently. It may be particularly relevant if you suffer from imbalance issues like vertigo.

Refer to Chapter 9 'Fundamentals of being in water' and Chapter 10 'Floating horizontally', in order to build confidence in walking through water and standing up independently from floating positions.

TIPS

- **The fear of failure**

This is a very real fear, and one I've encountered with many students who've either tried before or feel a strong pressure to succeed (put on either by themselves or by others).

TIPS

Refer to Chapter 5.3 'Ten tips to help you to prepare for the journey ahead' for suggestions on how to create a positive mindset.

5.2 CONQUERING YOUR FEARS

This may be easier said than done.

According to the science of neuroplasticity (referred to in Chapter 2 'You & this book'), anxiety and fear are ingrained in the deep inner part of the brain, and in a lot of cases there is little or no conscious control of it.

These feelings then project to the outer part of the brain (cortex), which leads to a 'fighting' within the brain of what is 'objective' versus 'subjective'. This means that although you may know *objectively* – or rationally – that you've no reason to panic (like when standing in shallow water), *subjectively* – or emotionally – your mind tells you otherwise.

You may need to spend some time working through the exercises of walking and floating in water depending on your degree of fear or phobia.

If you find that this internal battle is hard to overcome by yourself, it may be worth reaching out for professional help. I've had students who've really benefited from structuring their water sessions in between meeting a hypnotherapist or psychologist.

5.3 TEN TIPS TO HELP YOU TO PREPARE FOR THE JOURNEY AHEAD

Some of these tips elaborate on the five key steps to success listed in Chapter 2 'You & this book' which underpin the theory of neuroplasticity; that is, the ability of the brain to master a new skill later in life.

These can be useful even if you classify yourself as Swimmer B (beginner without fear) or Swimmer C (that lacks technique).

1. **Try to relax and remember to breathe.** The number one thing to remember to do in the water is RELAX! I know, it's easier said than done, but it can really make a world of difference. Not relaxing can lead to hyperventilation and rushing exercises, which in turn can lead to choking on water, frustration and the feeling of loss of control. Tension can also cause your muscles to contract, which means a heavier body; making it harder to float and to move.

    So, before starting any exercise, prepare yourself mentally to do it in slow motion or half the speed than you think, and take time to *breathe*. A student Nathan used to swim way too fast. His survival instinct caused him to rush every movement in the water due to a previous drowning experience.

2. **Stay positive.** The power of the mind shouldn't be underestimated. Doubt or fear can stop your body from trying things. I've witnessed students who float perfectly several times consecutively. If any self-doubt then enters their head, they're suddenly convinced that they can't do it (and subsequently fail to float successfully the next time).

    Always remind yourself of the level you started at. You'll have good days and bad days when practising. It's important to recall how far you've come. Every time you're in the water you'll increase your practical experience, just like every time you get behind the steering wheel when learning how to drive.

    Set yourself goals and **keep a diary** if you wish. This can help you to track how you're progressing at every session to maintain self-efficacy (that is, the belief in your own ability to achieve a task) and to recognise your rewards (referring to Chapter 2.4 'The theory of neuroplasticity').

    If – or when – water gets into your body (and it can happen to the best of swimmers), it's easy to feel demotivated. Many of my students tell me they evaluate the success of a session by the volume of water they've swallowed! It can be difficult to forget when you choke on water, and it's physically uncomfortable when water enters the nose. Try to stay positive and accept that it's a side effect of learning; similar to falling down when learning to ski. Refer to Chapter 6.7 'Equipment to wear' for advice on how to manage water intake.

3. **Identify if you're in the right mood** to learn. Being open to learning will be key to your success. A student James had just broken up with his long-term partner a few hours before our lesson together. He wasn't in the right mindset to learn and decided to stop his lesson as he couldn't focus properly. If you can't concentrate for whatever reason, there's no point trying to learn as it'll affect the quality of your practice (referring to Chapter 2.4 'The theory of neuroplasticity'). This will only lead to frustration in addition to no positive result.

    Identifying if you're in the right mood may be difficult, depending on how self-disciplined you are! Find the best time of day and day(s) of the week that work best for you.

    It'll be important to ensure that you keep to a regular routine and only excuse yourself from practice in very unusual circumstances. Ladies, consider your menstrual cycle when planning practice time so that you don't risk losing momentum.

4. **Be patient with yourself.** Try not to imagine how you'd cope without training aids. From my experience it's tempting for students to pre-occupy themselves with that thought and skipping too far ahead mentally can lead to frustration and the fear of failure. Take it in baby steps and trust in the process.

    Reaching your goals may take some time, and this can be underestimated. You'll need to allow repetition and practice to take hold in your brain (referring to Chapter 2.4 'The theory of neuroplasticity'). This is particularly important if you recognise that you've certain bad habits that need to be corrected. **The longer you've swum with a fault, the longer it might take** to unlearn and relearn the right technique.

    The time will come when you'll be swimming independently but it's crucial to follow the systematic progressions to get you there.

If you start to get frustrated, mix up exercises of what you *can* do in between the activities you're finding difficult. This will help to maintain your morale and motivation.

5. **Be prepared for lots of repetition.** Try to avoid the temptation of moving onto the next exercise before you've mastered the previous one. There's a method behind my progressions that involves working through skills in isolation before building upon them.

   For example, if you haven't yet learnt how to breathe comfortably, there's no point in learning strokes as it'll be too much for you to have to think about and coordinate altogether.

   I often give the analogy of learning to drive: would you try to park a car if you don't yet know how to use the gears? The brain requires experience and repetition before actions become automated and habitual.

6. **Don't compare yourself with others.** I stopped running sessions with multiple students together when I realised that it's human nature to judge your abilities against others. I used to teach pairs of students; some were siblings, some were couples, some were friends or colleagues. Ultimately everyone progresses at different speeds and has different strengths and weaknesses – *even when starting at the same level.* Stay focused on yourself and your own journey.

7. **Try not to dwell on the fact that you didn't do this when you were younger.** I've lost count of the number of times that a student has told me remorsefully; "I just wish I'd done this as a kid!" Everyone has regrets. I wish I'd learnt to ski when I was a kid. Focus on the present and your imminent future in the water world. A student Grace learnt from scratch as a very fearful beginner at the age of eighty-two: it really is never too late!

8. **Accept that you'll make mistakes.** Learning to swim as an adult can be more difficult than some people think. A student Sally was an ambitious high-flying business woman. She told me that she was used to excelling in every aspect of her life, both professionally and personally, and really struggled to accept that she was making mistakes and progressing slower than her usual fast pace of learning.

Keep in mind **you may find some exercises harder than others**. But remember that you can learn better through making mistakes rather than getting things right first time.

Try not to over-analyse your performance. This can lead to over-thinking exercises and making them unnecessarily complicated.

9. If you become tired or struggle with coordination but still wish to continue practising, **walk the exercise** instead of trying to do it horizontally. This builds in recovery periods for your muscles and helps to progressively work on your multi-tasking skills.

    If you're Swimmer A (beginner with fear), you may find it easier to **swim towards the pool edge or steps**. It'll help you to feel safer and to build your confidence. Swimming along the long length of a pool may seem endless.

10. Before you finish your self-practice, do something in the water that you perform well at. This will help to **complete your session feeling positive and motivated for your next session**.

6: GETTING READY: PRACTICALITIES

6.1 WHERE TO SWIM

It's important to choose the right waterway where you'll feel comfortable to practise. I suggest returning to the same familiar environment for every session. Changing your surroundings too early in the learning process can throw you mentally and might cause you to regress in confidence. Humans are creatures of habit; my students tend to use the same changing room every time – it provides a sense of reassurance and feeling of being in control. It's also (almost) comforting to taste the same pool water!

I strongly recommend choosing a **swimming pool.**

Advantages of a swimming pool:

- Consistent water temperature.

- Water clarity.

- No hidden hazards, compared to a river or ocean with rips for example.

- A recreational/walking lane (usually closest to the pool edge). Check with your pool if you aren't sure where it is, or if it's only open at designated times. This lane creates a dedicated area for those who don't wish to swim laps. It's perfect to get familiar with being in water, i.e. to walk through water, breathe and float.

- Easy access into the water, usually via a set of steps or a ladder.

- Depth markers so it's clear where you can and can't stand. Remember to consider your height to mouth level and to not head level.

6.2 FACTORS TO CONSIDER WHEN CHOOSING A SWIMMING POOL

- **Indoor vs outdoor.** This depends on personal preference as well as weather conditions. Swimming in the rain shouldn't be an issue (you'll be getting wet anyway) but thunderstorms do present a safety risk. Refer to Chapter 6.6 'Swimwear' for information on how to protect your skin from the sun if you choose to swim outdoors.

- **Salty water vs chlorinated.** Salty water boosts buoyancy which means you'll find it easier to stay afloat and have the water support you. This means if you ultimately plan to only swim in chlorinated water, salty water would provide a false sense of confidence. However if you plan to eventually swim in open water, then getting used to this extra buoyancy in the controlled environment of a salt water swimming pool can help to prepare you.

- **Heated vs unheated.** This again depends on personal preference. It's crucial to feel comfortable. If you're cold, you might rush exercises. It might also discourage you from returning next time! A heated pool would be recommended if you start at a very basic level and aren't moving too much to begin with. Public swimming pools tend to be heated to around 28°C (82°F). I'm fortunate enough to run lessons at hydrotherapy pools where the temperature sits between 31 – 35°C (88° – 95°F) which is ideal for beginners.

- **25m (standard) vs 50m (Olympic) length.** 25m length is recommended to start with as it'll be much less daunting. You can transition to 50m length when you're ready to extend your distance. You might have access to a private pool (e.g. in an apartment complex) which could be shorter than 25m. This is fine for the early stages. However you'll probably feel ready to transition to a longer pool as you get more proficient and can swim longer lengths. Keep in mind that smaller pools may mean more waves due to backsplash, even if you're the only person in the water. A student Mia was prone to motion sickness and found the water in a smaller pool too choppy for her.

- **The colour of the pool floor tiles.** This may or may not be a consideration for you. If you have a fear of water, you may prefer to choose a pool with bright tiles. Light blue tiles can help to calm some nervous beginners. Dark colours can make a pool feel unwelcoming and deep.

- **Natural lighting.** Again, this may or may not be a consideration for you. An indoor pool with plenty of windows (or an outdoor pool) may have a positive impact on your mood and confidence in the water.

This book is written with the intention that all exercises are undertaken in a swimming pool.

There are of course alternative waterways if you prefer.

Rock pools are outdoor unheated tidal pools near beaches. Suitable if you're Swimmer B (without fear) or Swimmer C (that lacks technique). If you have the aspiration to get 'beach confident', then rock pools provide a useful transitional environment to the open water, because you can get familiar with moving through salty water without rips and waves to contend with. It's especially great to build confidence and skills in treading water.

ALERT

Be aware that due to their natural habitat, floors of rock pools may be uneven, slippery or sharp and the water may still be choppy depending on how close they are located to the ocean. I'd therefore recommend proceeding with caution if you're Swimmer A (beginner with fear).

Beaches should only be used if you're Swimmer B (without fear) or Swimmer C (that lacks technique) and able to tread water. Refer to Chapter 15.4 for more guidance on open water swimming. If you consider yourself to be a weak swimmer but still prefer to practise at a beach, choose a shallow sheltered bay where you can safely stand and be protected from waves and rips. Swimmers at a beach should swim between the red and yellow flags (in Australia), never swim alone and always adhere to warning signs.

Spas are an alternative if you're Swimmer A (beginner with fear) and feel the shallow end of a pool is not shallow enough for you. I've taught lessons in a spa before, to build a student's confidence in floating and kicking in the same spot. The extra warm temperature of the water and smaller enclosed space can help people to relax and feel supported. Be aware though that bubbles generated from a pump can disorient, so it's better to use the spa when the pump isn't in operation – and ideally when it's not being used by others!

6.3 WHEN TO SWIM

- As a learner, you'll benefit most from an **environment which is reasonably quiet and calm**. That means identifying a time when there's less likely to be kids or swim schools operating which create turbulence in the water and a noisy environment. Public pools usually have a timetable with scheduled activities. Winter is in fact one of the best times to learn; when lanes are generally much quieter.

- If you're planning to visit the venue by yourself, it may also be worth researching when there are **lifeguards** on duty for peace of mind. If you're very nervous you may wish to bring a **buddy** along, who can watch out for you and support you. Choose that person carefully; they need to be a good swimmer, patient and non-judgmental.

- **Allow enough time for your food to digest** beforehand; your stomach will otherwise feel very heavy in the water and it can be uncomfortable to move around. Chewing gum whilst in the water isn't recommended as it's a choking hazard.

- If you're concerned about straining a muscle, **warm up beforehand with stretches** either on land or in the water at standing depth.

- **Injuries** should be treated on a case by case basis. If you run the risk of getting an infection or incurring a more severe injury, consider postponing your practice. Be mindful that waterproof plasters may not stick well to your skin depending on their quality.

- **Ladies can still swim during a period** provided a tampon is worn to collect the menstrual fluid before it leaves the body.

6.4 WHAT TO PACK

- **Swimwear**

- **Towel**

- **Goggles**

- **Training aids**

- **Toiletries** (including make-up remover and a hydrating skin moisturiser if needed)

- **Bottle of water.** Learning how to swim is thirsty work – even if you think you've drunk enough of the pool water by accident! It's naturally difficult to be aware of how much your body sweats when you're already immersed in water, so keep yourself hydrated to avoid muscle cramps and any dizziness.

- A pair of open-toed flat **sandals** (with good grip for anti-slippage). They are the easiest type of footwear to get in and out of quickly and safely when walking to and from the pool. They may also be useful to shower in, depending on the cleanliness of the bathroom facilities!

- **Spare change** (if the changing room lockers and/or showers are coin operated).

- **Sunscreen** if swimming outdoor.

6.5 WHAT TO KNOW

- Familiarise yourself with **where the changing rooms and toilets** are.

- Be aware of the **pool rules** (e.g. no glass containers); these should be signposted.

- If it's requested that you rinse before entering the water, **put on your swimming costume first** before doing so. It can otherwise be difficult to change into it after a shower with moist skin.

- **Check the pool depths** (which should be clearly signposted) so you know where you can and cannot stand. Know your limitations; go only where you feel confident/capable.

- **Introduce yourself to the staff/lifeguards** if you're visiting the pool alone. They can help to answer any questions you may have.

- To avoid the possibility of what's called 'lane rage', **check the lane signage**. They indicate the designated speed, swimming direction, and sometimes the only permissible stroke(s) in each lane.

NOTES

The lane signage indicating relative speeds is quite subjective and of course open to individual interpretation! **Observe the current swimmers** *in the water (if any) and what speed they're swimming at, so you can identify which lane is appropriate for you to use at your level.*

- The **black lines on the pool floor** provide a guide to keep you moving straight in one direction, similar to the painted white lines on a road when driving. The end of the black line is in a T shape to signal to swimmers that they are approaching the end of the lane. This is useful when swimming on your front.

- There may be a **line of flags suspended across the ceiling**. It signals to swimmers that they are five metres from the end of the lane. This is useful when swimming on your back.

An example of a 25 metre public pool (view from above)

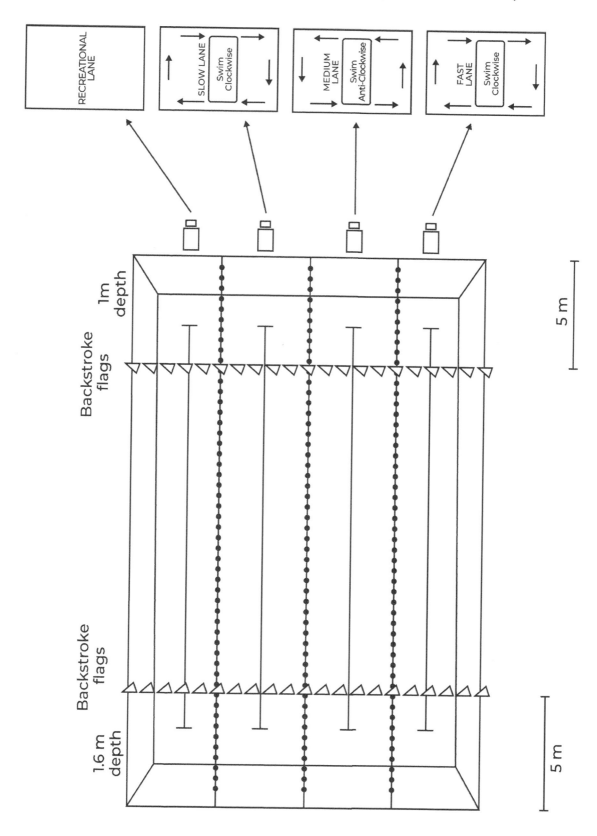

6.6 SWIMWEAR

It's important to wear proper swimwear in the water and not 'regular' clothing! I have encountered many students arriving for their first swimming lesson wearing gym gear. Cotton material soaks up the water and becomes very heavy and restrictive to move in.

Chlorine resistant costumes last much longer than other swim fabrics. **Skin-tight** apparel minimizes resistance (or 'drag') in the water, making it much easier to move in. Boardshorts are loose fitting and can act like a parachute in the water.

Having said this, the most important thing is that you feel comfortable in your swimwear. And remember that once you're in the water, nobody will pay any attention to what you're wearing.

Sun tops (otherwise known as 'rash shirts' or 'rashies') can protect your skin from sun exposure. Look out for the label stating their ultraviolet protection factor (UPF) rating (for protection from the sun's UVA and UVB rays) if you're planning to swim outdoors. The higher the rating the better, with 50+ being excellent. Sun tops are also a great option for those who are body conscious. Just ensure you find a size that is reasonably skin-tight; it'll otherwise create resistance in your movements.

Wetsuits are great for cold water environments. Water that becomes trapped between your skin and suit is heated by your body, providing a warm layer of insulation. (When possible I have a warm shower after putting a wetsuit on, to instantly create this!) Be mindful however that a wetsuit provides extra buoyancy, similar to the effect of being in salty water. If you don't plan to ultimately swim wearing one on a regular basis, then it would be wiser to wear regular swimwear to get used to your body's own natural buoyancy.

Taking care of swimwear

- Rinse with fresh water after use (you can handwash from time to time with mild soap).
- Dry out of direct sunlight.
- Apply sunscreen carefully as oil/lotion can deteriorate the fabric.

Ladies swimwear

There are countless designs on the market, including a vast range of back strap styles. What's important is that you wear a *sturdy* one or two piece costume. String bikinis aren't practical to learn in – you don't want the distraction of constantly having to adjust your swimwear! The two key considerations will be type of bust support (e.g. full foam cups or shelf bra, etc) and leg height (e.g. high or low cut, shorts, etc).

Examples of a one-piece costume

(Also available in maternity fit)

Different components of a two-piece costume

Cross trainer top or tankini top

Crop top

Pant

Boy leg shorts (skin tight)

Mid thigh shorts (skin tight)

Knee length shorts (skin tight) "jammers"

Cross-trainer sets can be worn for land exercise (e.g. at the gym) as well as in the water. They provide an active fit and therefore generally have better support. Tankini sets are just for use in the water but can be easier to get in and out of.

Sun tops

Otherwise known as 'rash shirts' or 'rashies'. These can be with or without front zips.

Watershorts

Otherwise known as 'boardshorts' or 'boardies'.

Watershort
(loose fit, short length)

Watershort
(loose fit, knee length)

Different components of modesty suits

Hood   Tunic (slim fit)   Pant (relaxed fit)   Dress (relaxed fit)   Legging

TIPS

I love wearing the swim legging for warmth in cold water or for skin protection when outdoors.

NOTES

Special notes for ladies:

- *Try to limit the amount of jewellery you wear. Dangly earrings and necklaces can be a safety hazard.*
- *Remove all make-up to maintain the condition of your goggles and avoid panda eyes. If you choose to wear a nose clip (refer to Chapter 6.7 'Equipment to wear'), moisturiser and foundation can make it difficult for it to grip well on your skin, so ensure you remove all cosmetics.*
- *You can still swim during a period if you wear a tampon.*

Mens swimwear

Skin-tight shorts

Brief or racer

Shorts (short length) "trunk"

Shorts (mid length) "mid jammers"

Shorts (knee length) "jammers"

Sun tops

Otherwise known as 'rash shirts' or 'rashies'. These can come in slim fit or loose fit.

Loose fitting shorts

Otherwise known as 'boardshorts' or 'boardies'.

Mid thigh length

Knee length

TIPS

If you prefer to wear loose fitting shorts, look for a pair with mesh inner briefs, to avoid wearing your underwear in the water, which is neither practical nor hygienic. Alternatively you could wear a swim brief or racer underneath loose fitting shorts.

NOTES

Special note for men:

- *If you have a long beard, tie it into a ponytail or twist it into a tight bun. This will stop it affecting your vision and balance.*

6.7 EQUIPMENT TO WEAR

Equipment to wear

EQUIPMENT TO WEAR	
Essential	**Optional**
Goggles	Cap*
	Nose clip
	Earplugs

*In some countries a cap may be obligatory to wear at public swimming pools.

Goggles

Definition: protective eyewear. *Referred to by some people as 'googles' or 'glasses'.*

Do you need them?
Yes I strongly recommend it.

Firstly, you'll have **clearer underwater visibility.** Generally people reflexively close their eyes when submerged but it's crucial to keep them open. It's otherwise like running with your eyes closed! How do you know where you are? Or where you are going? Or what is around you? You'll notice a huge difference in underwater visibility of objects with and without goggles – this will most certainly enhance your level of water confidence. If in doubt, try looking at your hands or feet underwater with and without goggles to compare the difference.

Secondly, you'll benefit from **eye protection.** Water may contain harmful bacteria and chlorine/salt that can cause your eyes to sting and redden.

ALERT

A student Gareth insisted on avoiding goggles even when wearing contact lenses. It's particularly important to wear eye protection as otherwise harmful bacteria can get trapped between your eyeball and contact lens. (It happened to me and the result is a nasty eye ulcer – fortunately I escaped permanent eye damage.) It's not ideal to wear contact lenses and goggles together due to this hygiene risk. Wearing prescription goggles is the best and safest solution for people with poor eyesight (I'm still resisting laser eye surgery!) Wearing non-prescription goggles with poor eyesight will be detrimental to your water confidence.

NOTES

Some argue that they don't want to get dependent on wearing goggles, in the event that in an emergency they would panic in the water without them. For example if they fall into water by accident. This is a valid point, and by all means it would be a good idea to get familiar in water without goggles – once you've built your confidence.

Choosing the right goggles:

Once you start shopping around you'll notice there's a huge range of different goggles on the market, all with various technical icons on the packaging – it can be quite overwhelming. Simply put, you'll be looking for something that is comfortable to wear, easy to use, and most importantly, doesn't leak. Generally, brands these days include UV protection as a standard feature. If you're planning to ultimately swim outdoors, then look out for ones with polarized lenses that reduce the glare and reflections of the sun on the water.

NOTES

There seems to be a level of acceptance by some people that goggles will leak. I've taught students who I can immediately tell are used to wearing leaking goggles, as they're still in the habit of swimming with their eyes shut even when wearing a perfectly fitting pair of goggles that are keeping their eyes dry!

I can't state strongly enough how important it is to try goggles on before purchase, to ensure that you get the right pair to fit your face shape. If possible, go to a shop which has goggles on display for you to try on.

Goggle fitting test

Push them against your face *without using the strap* and then remove your hands holding them in place. If they don't fall off immediately, they're a good fit for your face shape and will most likely not leak.

1. Types

There are three types of lens: clear, mirrored and tinted. A clear pair will greatly enhance your confidence with getting your face wet. Mirrored and tinted goggles can make the water appear dark and uninviting, particularly if the pool is indoor. I've witnessed a huge leap in students' confidence – and their willingness to submerge – after switching from dark to transparent pairs.

There are three types of nose bridges: single inbuilt (fixed size), multiple separate (different attachable sizes) and single adjustable size. If you have a high or flat nose, the latter two types are more suitable for you. They are illustrated below.

Goggles with separate attachable bridges of different widths

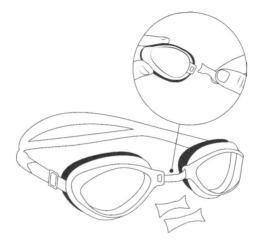

Goggles with one notched nose bridge that can be adjusted to different widths

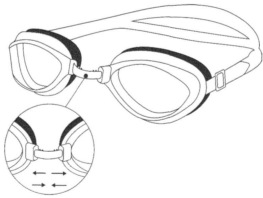

There are three types of strap adjustments; a buckle, a lever and a push button. Each have their pros and cons.

STRAP TYPE	ADVANTAGE	DISADVANTAGE
Buckle	• Quick to adjust.	• Strap is smooth: so the buckle can slide around, loosening the strap.
Lever	• Strap has grooves, providing a better grip.	• Can be fiddly to adjust.
Push button	• Strap has grooves, providing a better grip.	• A push button can sometimes stick.

TIPS

Put goggles on first, and then adjust the strap to get a comfortable fit.

NOTES

The strap is simply to hold the goggles in place – not to provide the seal. So try to avoid the temptation of pulling the strap too tight around your head as it can otherwise leave deep red marks on your skin and possibly give you a headache.

Buckle on the side

To tighten: pull the ends of the strap like this:

Or pull the buckle towards your ears like this:

Buckle at the back

To tighten: pull the ends of the strap like this:

Push button or lever

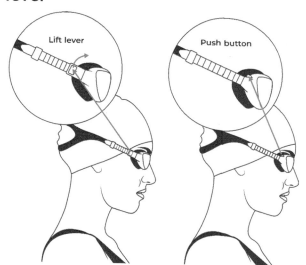

Strap with a 'split yoke'

Otherwise known as a double band. This is essentially two straps that can secure goggles better at the back of your head (you can wear one strap above and one below the back of your head/ponytail). I prefer the split yoke because a single strap can tend to slip down towards the back of your neck over time.

2. Sizes

If you're not used to wearing glasses, you may find goggles a little claustrophobic, as the lenses can hug at your eye sockets. Masks are a great alternative because they provide wider vision and can feel more comfortable to wear.

Example of a mask (by Zoggs)

If you have a smaller or narrower face, there are junior and women's goggles that might suit your face shape better.

Putting goggles on

1. Put on your cap first (if you choose to wear one – see below section on caps). This is because if you have issues with your goggles whilst swimming and need to take them off for any reason, you won't need to first remove your cap every time.

2. Check which way the goggles should be worn so you don't wear them upside down. This can be done by looking for a brand name or logo which is usually printed on either the strap or nose bridge.

3. Place the goggles over your eyes and push them slightly against your face. You should feel a gentle suction which indicates that you have a good seal to avoid leakage.

4. You can then pull the strap around so it sits at the *back of your head* and *above your ears* (not at the base of your neck).

Taking care of goggles

*   Avoid touching the lens. Generally, brands these days claim anti-fog on their packaging. Fogging occurs due to one of two reasons. Firstly, when your skin temperature is warmer than that of the goggles – similar to the windscreen of a warm car on a cold day. If this is the case, either cool down your skin by splashing water on your face, or warm up your goggles by dipping them in the water. Secondly, when the topical anti-fog film coating on the inside lens has been removed (either due to wear and tear or finger rubbing). If this is the case, apply anti-fog liquid to the lens or simply buy a new pair of goggles.

*   Rinse them in fresh water after use and then air dry (e.g. by hanging them on a doorknob or tap). Leaving them in your bag could mean they then dry misshapen...which means they'll not seal well against your face next time and lead to leakage.

*   Don't twist or fold them.

*   Don't store them under direct sunlight. Store them in a protective carry case or storage pouch. (This may already be included in your original goggles packaging.)

TIPS

Never spit or rub the inside lens of your goggles! You'll remove the topical layer of anti-fog film and cause irreversible damage.

Caps

Definition: headwear to keep hair away from your face. *Referred to by some people as: 'shower caps' or 'hats'.*

Do you need one?
This depends on your hairstyle and personal preferences. Caps enable **unobstructed vision**.

If you can't see properly whilst in the water due to wet hair across your eyes, you'll spend more time wiping your hair away from your face rather than using your hands and arms to swim.

Taking goggles on and off is much easier. Without a cap, you can get your hair tangled in the goggle strap and risk hair breakage.

It can also **protect your scalp** from the harshness of the sun (if outdoors).

Advantages of a rubber/silicone/latex cap

- To **keep hair as dry** as possible **and protected** from chlorine, salty water and the harshness of the sun (if outdoors). (This can be particularly important if your hair is dyed.) There are no guarantees on keeping your hair completely dry but this type of cap will undoubtedly give a better chance than cloth. Ensure you tuck ALL hair inside. Use a hair tie (if you have long hair) to tie a ponytail in the middle of the back of your head. You can either spin it into a bun or plait it (to avoid knots after swimming). Avoid using bobby pins or hard plastic clips in your hair as these can rip the cap.

- There are caps shaped discreetly with **ear flaps to block water** from entering (Zoggs sell a great one called the Ultra Fit).

- This type of cap can double up as a **carry bag for your wet costume** after swimming!

- This type of cap can also **retain heat**. I actually wear two of these on top of each other when swimming in open water.

Advantages of a material/spandex/cloth cap

- Can be **more comfortable** to wear if you find the rubber type tugs at your hair.

- Can **feel less tight** around your head compared with the rubber type, which can give some people a headache.

NOTES

From my experience cloth caps are generally popular amongst men who aren't concerned about keeping their hair dry or protected and simply wish to keep hair away from their face.

TIPS

- *I wet my hair under the shower first, so that my hair soaks up clean water rather than the chemicals in pool water. I then protect it by coating it with hair conditioner, before putting on a rubber cap. This provides an extra layer of protection and also makes my hair less knotty after swimming.*
- *If you'd rather avoid wearing a cap, you could use clips to keep your hair away from your face. A cap would be much more straightforward though, rather than fiddling with clips.*

NOTES

Similar to swimwear, the most important thing is that you feel comfortable. A student Maria suffered from alopecia and was bald. She didn't need a cap but preferred wearing one to feel less self-conscious. A student Alistair was always used to wearing a cap (professionally as a nurse in theatre) and so didn't feel right without wearing one in the water too – even though he had very short hair which didn't obstruct his vision! Conversely, a student Felicity who was a complete beginner, refused to wear a cap as she thought she'd feel like an imposter looking like she knew how to swim when she couldn't yet.

Choosing the right cap

1. **Types:**

   There are two *feels* of caps; rubber/silicone/latex and material/spandex/cloth. I say 'feel' as there are technical differences between these types; however these won't be important to you for your purpose of getting water confident.

2. Sizes:

There are two sizes of adult caps; standard and long hair (also suitable for large heads).

TIPS

- *If you've a **large head or long/thick hair** choose a long hair cap that has extra stretch. If you get a standard size cap which is too small for either your hair or your head, it'll start to ride up and fall off during your swim. There are also tall shaped caps for those with long **Afro-textured hair**.*

- *For long hair, braid it beforehand so it's not so knotty afterwards.*

- *A ponytail should be tied in the middle of the back of your head (rather than low or high). If you've goggles with a double band, secure them in place above and below the ponytail.*

- *For thick or big hair, try tying your hair into two bunches to spread out the volume, rather than one large ponytail.*

Putting a cap on

1. Always put the cap on first before goggles, this is particularly important when using a cap with discreet ear flaps in order to ensure a good seal around your ears.

2. Look for the crease or fold in the cap and wear it so this runs down the middle of your crown. Alternatively look for the logo to wear on the side of your head. This will prevent the cap from riding up and falling off. Hold the cap open with your hands from the inside before you put it on.

3. You can either put the cap behind your ears or cover your ears completely. Half covering your ears can lead to water blockage in the ears.

How to put a cap on

TIPS

Make sure that your cap isn't in between your forehead skin and goggles. This is to ensure a good seal of your goggles against your face to avoid leakage.

Taking care of your cap

Rinse it under fresh water and hang dry so it doesn't dry stuck together.

Nose clips

Definition: accessory to stop water from entering your nostrils. *Referred to by some people as: 'nose plugs' – but **please note that they should never be inserted into the nostrils!***

Do you need one?
Yes, if you struggle to master the correct breath control (refer to Chapter 9 'Fundamentals of being in water') and find water entering your nose. Nose clips allow you to progress without the distraction or unpleasantness of water entering.

NOTES

- *If you're apprehensive about getting dependent on wearing one, remember you can transition away from them with time, just like goggles.*

- *You may need to wear nose clips with a centre line snorkel (refer to Chapter 6.8 'Equipment to use').*

Choosing the right nose clip

1. Types

There are two main types: plastic and wired.

Example of plastic nose clip with carry case (by Zoggs)

Example of wired nose clip (by Speedo)

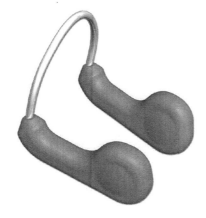

2. Sizes

They are all labelled as universal fit however the wired ones provide a tighter grip so are more suitable for those with wider or flatter noses.

Putting a nose clip on

- Start *at the top* of your nose bridge and then slide it down towards your nostrils. Avoid widening the clip too much before wearing it, as it'll loosen the grip. It should sit on top of your nostrils and *not inserted inside* them.

How to put a nose clip on

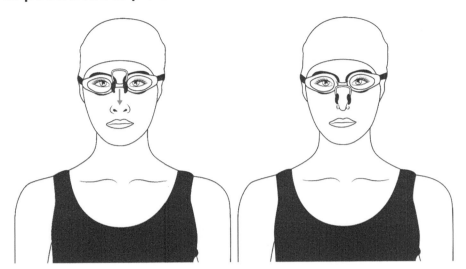

1. Test the seal by trying to inhale only through your nose above water. If you can't, then no water should be able to enter.

TIPS

- *If you drop them on the pool floor and are at standing depth, use your toes to pick them up – it's a lot easier!*
- *Remove any moisturizer/make-up/suntan lotion from the skin of your nose to ensure a good grip. If you find it slipping off during your practice, keep your towel close by to dry your nose and nose clip before putting it on again.*
- *Ladies, you could hang your nose clip around your swimming costume shoulder strap when not using it (if it secures well).*

Ear plugs

Definition: accessory to stop water from entering the ears.

Do you need them?
Yes, if you have issues with water entering your ears. This is an inevitable side-effect of swimming and the water will eventually drain out.

If you're sensitive to this, or are prone to ear infections, you'll be anxious and not move your head correctly which can lead to incorrect body positioning.

A student Alex suffered from bad ear infections, so he chose to wear both ear plugs and a cap with ear flaps to really maximise the seal.

Choosing the right ear plugs

1. **Types**

    There are two main types: firm ones that you either screw in or push in, and soft ones that are malleable to fit your ear canal.

    Example of screw in ear plugs (by Speedo) that block both water and sound

    Example of push in ear plugs with carry case (by Zoggs) that block water but not sound

    Example of malleable putty ear plugs with carry case (by Zoggs)

2. **Sizes**

    There are no variations in size.

6.8 EQUIPMENT TO USE

Fortunately swimming is a sport that doesn't require expensive equipment, unlike my husband's new kitesurfing hobby!

Getting water confident involves multi-tasking and coordination. Training aids serve to break down your learning into separate core elements and are useful for *any* skill level of swimmer.

It's normal to feel a little reluctant to use them, for fear of becoming dependent on them.

As you progress through the exercises, try not to get pre-occupied on *when* you'll move away from the aids. If you follow the steps progressively, you'll naturally be able to transition away from them as you grow in competence and confidence. Just trust in the method!

Below is a list of my recommendations.

TIPS

It may be worth checking if your pool already has training aids like kickboards and noodles available for you to borrow.

EQUIPMENT TO USE	
Essential	**Optional**
Kickboard	Noodle
	Snorkel
	Pullbuoy (advanced)
	Fins (advanced)

Kickboard

Definition: a rectangular piece of foam with a curved or pointed top. It's a flotation aid to assist with your upper body.

Do you need one?
Yes, it's by far the most popular training aid because it's so versatile. It's also easier to control your balance and movements in the water.

There are certain exercises where the kickboard can be substituted with a noodle instead; this will be indicated in the relevant sections.

Choosing the right kickboard

1. **Types**

    There are two main types: with and without handles. The former is useful if you're not yet comfortable or ready to get your face wet, or to strengthen kicking.

    Example of a kickboard with handles (by Zoggs)

    Example of a kickboard without handles (by Speedo)

2. **Sizes**

    There are two different sizes: adult and junior. (There are also smaller adult kickboards but they're more suitable for advanced level swimmers.)

NOTES

Junior kickboards are not suitable for adults! I wouldn't recommend using your child's kickboard. They're much lighter and won't support your body weight so you'll feel less stable. It's similar to trying to learn how to cycle on a kid's bike.

How to use a kickboard on your front

Hold it with arms outstretched; fingers on top and thumbs underneath.

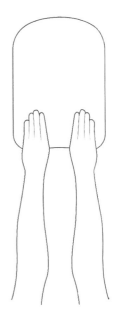

Alternative way to use a kickboard on your front

If you have a big head or large arms, you may find the above position difficult. Hold the kickboard on the sides instead with arms outstretched. (Try to hold it towards the bottom as illustrated below so you're not too dependent on it.)

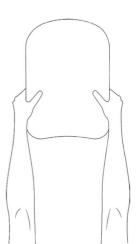

How not to use a kickboard on your front!

Do not place your hand ON TOP of the kickboard! You'll push down on it, causing your upper body to lift and lower body to drop. This will mean your body won't be horizontal (as it should be).

How to use a kickboard on your back (view from above)

Hold it at the sides against your chest with elbows pointing out. Hugging (wrapping your arms around) the kickboard will cause you to roll around and feel unstable.

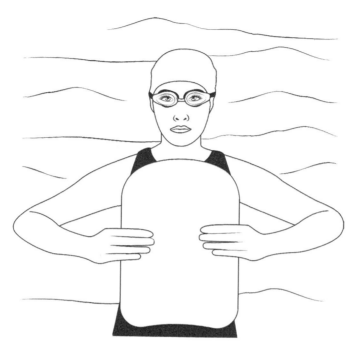

Noodle

Definition: a long foam cylinder. It's a flotation aid to maintain balance whilst vertical or maintain buoyancy when horizontal (on either front or back). *Referred to by some people as a 'woggle'.*

Do you need one?
This depends on which exercises are relevant to you in this book.

There are certain exercises where a noodle can be substituted with one or two kickboards instead; this will be indicated in the relevant sections.

TIPS

Since a noodle is much less discreet to carry compared with a kickboard, check if your pool stocks them to borrow from.

Choosing the right noodle

1. **Types**

   There are two types; solid foam, and with a hole.

Noodle with solid foam

This can absorb more water, making them less buoyant and prone to the foam material disintegrating faster over time.

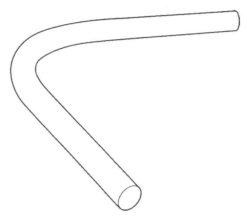

Noodle with a hole

I personally prefer the type with a hole, as they provide more buoyancy by holding air inside.

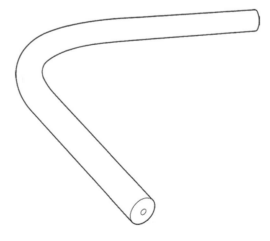

2. **Sizes**

   They usually come in one standard length.

How to hold a noodle when standing

Hold a noodle with arms outstretched and apart; fingers on top and thumbs underneath.

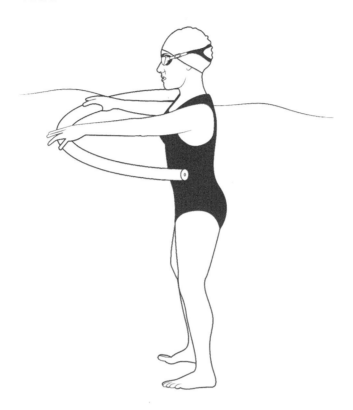

How to use a noodle on your front (basic level)

Place it under your arms.

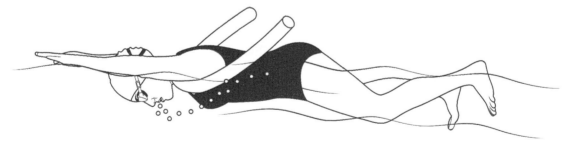

How to use a noodle on your front (advanced level)

Place it across your hips.

For some exercises in this book you'll also be holding a kickboard. Below is a breakdown of the steps to use a kickboard and noodle at the same time.

How to use a noodle and a kickboard on your front

1. Push the noodle down with one hand (so it's across your hips) whilst holding the kickboard with the other hand.

2. Lean forward to raise legs.

3. Place your second hand on the kickboard.

If you struggle, get onto your front first (face down) then push the noodle down to your hips.

TIPS

You may find securing the noodle under your hips is easier if you have a belly! That's because your belly will stop the noodle riding up towards your chest when horizontal.

NOTES

How to use a noodle on your back

Place it across your back and under your armpits.

Consider using two noodles if you need extra support.

- *Always make sure your body is leaning against the middle of the noodle rather than towards one end, otherwise it's prone to slip off.*

TIPS

Taking care of a noodle

Rinse under fresh water and leave somewhere well ventilated to air dry; it can otherwise grow mould.

Snorkel

Definition: a breathing aid used on your front only.

Do you need one?
This depends on your skill level and needs.

If you're Swimmer A (beginner with fear) and are **really struggling to master a front float**. You can practise balancing on your front and standing up without rushing or panicking in fear of running out of air.

If you're Swimmer B (without fear) or Swimmer C (that lacks technique), a snorkel can **help you to focus on different skill areas without the interruption of inhaling above water** e.g. stroke correction on freestyle.

If you're Swimmer C (that lacks technique) and are ready **to build stamina** in the water, you can increase your swimming distance and/or treading water time without having to stop if you get breathless.

If you **plan to go snorkelling and wish to get your own snorkel kit for hygiene reasons**, you can get familiar with using one in the 'safe' environment of a pool before heading to the open water. A student Peter did this, and pretended he was looking for something he had lost at the bottom of the public pool!

NOTES

- *Breath control whilst wearing a snorkel involves inhaling through mouth and exhaling through mouth only.*
- *Adults can often be reluctant to use a snorkel, for fear of losing confidence and skills with the correct breath control. I always recommend mixing up your practice with and without a snorkel in order to avoid becoming dependent on it.*

ALERT

Never use a snorkel whilst on your back as water will enter the top of the tube.

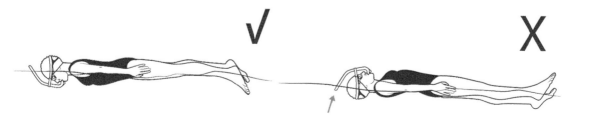

Choosing the right snorkel

1. Types

There are two types: a centre line snorkel (tube only) specifically for swim training and a recreational snorkel kit (mask and tube) for observing marine life.

2. Sizes

A centre line snorkel is worn in front of your face and has a long tube. You can wear it together with goggles.

A recreational snorkel is worn on the side of your face and has a shorter tube. It comes together with a mask.

A centre line snorkel (with nose clip)

The advantage of a centre line snorkel is that the tube is longer and therefore sits higher above the water level so you're less likely to catch water if you move your head from side to side.

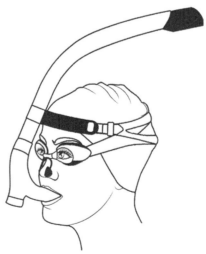

NOTES

You may also need a nose clip if you find water entering your nose. This clip may or may not be included in the packaging of a centre line snorkel.

TIPS

The easiest order to put on your equipment is: goggles, centre line snorkel, (then nose clip if applicable).

A recreational snorkel kit

The advantage of a recreational snorkel kit is that the mask automatically seals your nose without the need to wear a separate nose clip.

However the tube is shorter which increases the chance of the top of the tube submerging.

If this happens, push the tube back towards your ear to raise the height of the tube when face down. Alternatively, use a kickboard to prevent your head from dipping too low in the water.

TIPS

Putting a snorkel on

It can take time to get familiar with wearing one. This is completely normal. The two challenges are: wearing more on your face (and possibly feeling a little claustrophobic) and getting used to a different way of breathing (if you learnt the correct breath control).

1. If you have a centre line snorkel, put goggles on first, then the snorkel (and then the nose clip if necessary).

    If you have a recreational snorkel kit, ensure there's a good seal of the mask underneath your nose.

    Adjust the strap so that it fits comfortably around the back of your head, just like a pair of goggles.

2. Ensure there's a complete seal of your lips around the whole mouthpiece – there's no need to grip it tightly with your teeth.

3. Inhale through your mouth (using tube) and exhale through your mouth (using tube).

HOME

It can take time to get used to breathing through a snorkel and this is completely normal. Try using it in the sink or bath at home. A student Max practised wearing this in his private office at work!

TIPS

- *Imagine the tube is like a giant straw, and you're sucking air through the tube rather than a drink.*
- *It's particularly important not to exhale through the nose whilst wearing a recreational snorkel mask, as your mask will steam up.*

It's useful to know how to resolve problems with water entering your equipment. This is particularly important in the event that you're not at standing depth to fix the problem easily!

Clearing a snorkel tube of water

This is due to either water entering from the top of the tube (i.e. you submerged too low) or via the mouthpiece (i.e. there wasn't a complete seal around the mouthpiece with your lips).

Inhale slowly through the tube with your mouth above water (carefully taking in air and not water) and then exhale sharply through the mouth. This will cause the trapped water to shoot out of the top of the tube thanks to the purge valve.

VIDEO

Clearing a snorkel mask of water

This is due to an ineffective seal between the mask and your face. Either your cap or hair is caught in between, creating a gap for water to enter.

Inhale through the tube with your mouth above water and exhale inside the mask through your nose to expel the water, whilst looking up from underwater and pushing the mask against your face with your hand.

Taking care of your snorkel

Give it a rinse under fresh water and leave somewhere well ventilated to dry; it can otherwise grow mould in the inside of the tube/mouthpiece.

Pullbuoy

Definition: a small, figure-eight shaped piece of foam. It's a flotation aid to assist with your lower body's buoyancy by raising your hips and eliminates the need to kick; so you can focus only on your upper body.

Do you need one?
Yes, if you're Swimmer C (that lacks technique).

It enables **stroke correction** (it can also be used with a snorkel on your front).

Squeezing it between your thighs **encourages a streamlined position** with your legs.

It strengthens upper body, **increasing core strength** by isolating strokes and/or breathing.

TIPS

- *If your lower body sinks when using a pullbuoy, you can kick a little to maintain your horizontal positioning.*
- *Try using it for the first time at standing depth, as it may take time to get used to it. If you feel unstable you can then simply let go of it between your legs and stand up.*

1. **Types**

   There is generally just one type.

2. **Sizes**

   There are two different shaped pullbuoys; one which has bulbs of equal size and the other which has bulbs of different sizes.

   Example of a pullbuoy with bulbs of equal size (by Zoggs)

Example of a pullbuoy with bulbs of different sizes (by Speedo)

How do I use it?

Place it between your thighs.

TIPS

If you have a pullbuoy with bulbs of different sizes, place it between your thighs with the bigger bulb pointing towards the pool floor to provide more buoyancy and support.

Fins

Definition: footwear to assist with flutter kicking. *Referred to by some people as: 'flippers'.*

Do you need them?
This depends on your skill level and needs.

If you're Swimmer A (beginner with fear) and have an excessive knee bend when flutter kicking, wearing fins can help **to correct the kick** by lengthening the leg movement and encouraging pointed toes (rather than flexing the ankles).

If you're Swimmer B (without fear) or Swimmer C (that lacks technique) and are ready to increase your swimming distance.

If you're Swimmer C (that lacks technique) and looking for **variation** in your practice.

NOTES

Fins aren't recommended if you already have a weak kick because they provide an enormous amount of propulsion with very little effort. They can therefore lead to a false sense of security if you've not first learnt how to propel without them.

Choosing the right fins

1. **Types**

   There are fins for snorkelling/diving and fins for swim training.

2. **Sizes**

   There are varying lengths of fin blades. Generally speaking the longer the blade, the easier it is to propel in the water. That's why scuba diving fins are long; for energy efficiency. I recommend short blade fins (as illustrated below).

   Example of swim training short blade fins (by Speedo)

 Be sure not to get too reliant on fins by mixing up your practice with and without wearing them. Fins are a great training aid but can encourage a lazy kick if over-used.

ALERT

Putting fins on

1. Sit on the pool edge or steps, or have a ladder to hold on to for balance.

2. There's no difference between left and right foot. They should fit snugly (like a hand glove) but not too tight that they hurt or rub your feet.

TIPS

- *Wetting your fins first makes them easier to put on.*
- *Put them on when close or in the water, as they're difficult to walk in on land!*
- *Practise standing from a float whilst wearing fins, before swimming in them. Make sure you bend your knees and allow plenty of time to stand, as otherwise you risk rushing, folding the fin and breaking it!*

NOTES

They may initially feel heavy to move in.

7: IDENTIFYING YOUR GOALS

There's a broad range of technical skills that you can learn in the water. Every individual will have their own goal(s) and definition of what success means to them. Perhaps it's to simply master floating. Or perhaps it's to swim a certain number of metres in freestyle. Or perhaps it's to be proficient at treading water.

Feel free to use this book as a reference guide and jump to chapters relevant to your specific objectives. Alternatively you can of course read it from cover to cover to broaden your knowledge across all competencies.

7.1 SUMMARY OF SKILLS TO SWIM AND SURVIVE

The skills covered in this book reflect the most popular areas that I'm requested by my adult students to teach.

Summary of skills to swim and survive

FLOATS	SWIMMING
*Front float to standing up *Back float to standing up *Rotate from front to back float *Tread water	*Kick on back Backstroke ('competitive') Backstroke ('survival') Breaststroke ('competitive') Breaststroke ('survival') Freestyle/front crawl

*Skills tagged with an asterisk above indicate the basic aquatic survival skills that I recommend mastering, even if you don't wish to progress to swimming any strokes.

7.2 SURVIVAL

Floating on front and back are the foundations before building any further skills in the water. Floating helps you to understand your buoyancy and to develop trust in the water to support your body. Even if you don't choose to progress to swimming, knowing what to do if your face gets wet (by way of a front float) will prevent you from panicking.

Once you know how to lie horizontally in the water, you can then start to move your arms and legs to propel you into swimming, following my sequence of progressions by stroke as detailed in the relevant chapters.

NOTES

I've met many students who've undertaken previous lessons with other swim schools that skip straight to swimming and have therefore never understood the basics of how to float and relax in the water. I cannot stress enough the importance of learning how to float first. It's like trying to run before you've first learnt how to stand up!

Linking your **floats through rotations** will help you to build your aptitude in controlling your body's balance in the water as well as getting confident with breath control. Knowing how to flip *from* front *to* back is important for water safety as you'll know what to do if you get tired or panicked on your front.

Treading water is a float whereby you're able to keep your mouth above the water level at depths where you can't stand. Mastering this skill will greatly increase your independence in the water so you don't have to limit yourself by only staying in areas where you can stand. It's particularly beneficial for swimming in any areas that aren't clearly signposted with depth markings, like at the beach or in a river.

Kicking on your back is the quickest and easiest way to swim from A to B, once you can back float. This is because swimming face up doesn't require you having to concentrate on breath control. You may choose to add arm movements however it's not crucial in order to move (and survive) on your back in the water.

7.3 SWIMMING STROKES

The **three 'mainstream' strokes** are freestyle ('front crawl'), breaststroke and backstroke, with deliberate omissions of sidestroke and butterfly. These latter strokes do have their own merits, however based on my own personal teaching experience, adult students are very rarely interested in learning them as people don't normally use these strokes in social swimming situations. That's to say there's a less compelling need to learn them to 'fit in' from a social perspective.

There are **two styles of backstroke** which I've evaluated below. Don't be put off by the term 'competitive' backstroke – it doesn't only relate to racing! Both variants can be swum slowly, with 'survival' backstroke providing a solution for those with neck or shoulder limitations.

There are also **two styles of breaststroke** which I've evaluated below. Again, don't be put off by the term 'competitive' breaststroke – it doesn't only relate to racing! In fact, it's easier to swim slower with 'competitive' breaststroke than 'survival' breaststroke as your body can generally glide further and for longer in between strokes and kicks.

I've not covered diving or tumble turns which are more applicable for the competitive swimmer. However, in Chapter 15 'Advanced skills' I do cover aspects of submerging and resurfacing in deep water, together with linking laps through (simpler) touch turns.

7.4 HOW TO CHOOSE BETWEEN THE STROKES

You may be wondering "Which stroke should I learn? I simply want to be able to swim *a stroke*." Which leads to the commonly asked question: which one is the simplest and quickest to master? You may've been told by others which stroke is the easiest to learn, but it really does depend on the individual. I'd recommend identifying this for yourself by asking the following questions.

Considerations on which stroke to learn:

- Are you more comfortable face down or face up?
  Work through Ex 10A 'Front float' and Ex 10B 'Back float' to find out.

- Do you prefer the (freestyle/backstroke) flutter kick or (breaststroke) whip kick?
  Work through Ex 14A 'Flutter kick on front with kickboard' or Ex 12A 'Flutter kick on back with kickboard' and Ex 13A 'Whip kick by pool edge/ ladder' to find out.

- Are you looking to conquer your fear of getting your face wet?
  If so, focus on learning a front stroke; either freestyle or breaststroke.

- Do you think you have bad coordination?
  If so, focus on learning competitive backstroke or survival backstroke. Neither require perfect coordination of arms and legs in order to swim it, nor the need to remember a certain breathing pattern.

The tables below evaluate the differences between each stroke from the perspective of an adult swim learner. As you can see, each stroke has its pros and cons.

Generally speaking, absolute beginners usually master backstroke first as you can breathe easy – unless you lack the confidence in back floating and are more comfortable face down.

For a lot of adults, freestyle is the aspiration, particularly in Australia. However, freestyle can be the most difficult stroke to learn because it demands crucial coordination and multi-tasking between arms, legs and breathing altogether.

 'Competitive' backstroke

'COMPETITIVE' BACKSTROKE		
IS IT EASY TO LEARN?	**BENEFITS**	**LIMITATIONS**
• Breathing: easy (always facing up). • Kicking: easy (flutter kick). • Coordination: easy (arms alternate and legs alternate).	• Can breathe as you wish. • A great recovery stroke if you get breathless or tired on your front. • Can alleviate back pain or tightness.	• Not recommended with a torn rotator cuff (injured shoulder) (consider reaching up to Ex 12B only or focus on survival backstroke). • No vision in the direction of travel. • If pregnant, seek medical advice before swimming on your back.

'Survival' backstroke

'SURVIVAL' BACKSTROKE		
IS IT EASY TO LEARN?	**BENEFITS**	**LIMITATIONS**
• Breathing: easy (always facing up). • Kicking**: difficult (whip kick). • Coordination: easy (arms and legs move all at once).	• Can breathe as you wish. • A great recovery stroke if you get breathless or tired on your front. • Can alleviate back pain or tightness. • Conserves body heat. • Can do the arm stroke even if you have shoulder limitations.	• Not recommended with bad knees or hips as this involves the whip kick. • No vision in the direction of travel. • If pregnant, seek medical advice before swimming on your back.

 'Competitive' breaststroke

'COMPETITIVE' BREASTSTROKE		
IS IT EASY TO LEARN?	**BENEFITS**	**LIMITATIONS**
• Breathing: medium (inhaling forwards and more often than freestyle). • Kicking**: difficult (whip kick). • Coordination: difficult (arms are paired and legs are paired).	• Less tiring as there's a glide phase where your whole body doesn't move. • Perceived as the graceful/ elegant stroke. • An option for people who've suffered a trauma and wish to conquer their fear of getting their face wet.	• Not recommended with bad knees or hips (consider replacing whip kick with flutter kick). • Not recommended with lower back conditions. • If pregnant, seek medical advice before attempting whip kick.

VIDEO

'Survival' breaststroke

'SURVIVAL' BREASTSTROKE		
IS IT EASY TO LEARN?	**BENEFITS**	**LIMITATIONS**
• Breathing: easy (always head above water). • Kicking**: difficult (whip kick). • Coordination: difficult (arms are paired and legs are paired).	• The only stroke where you're continually facing the direction of travel. • Full peripheral vision means it's popular to learn for enjoyment at the beach. • The only stroke if you wish to keep your hair dry and/or sunglasses on! • Has a social benefit in that you can talk and make eye contact with others whilst swimming. • Can breathe as you wish.	• Not recommended with bad knees or hips (consider replacing whip kick with flutter kick). • Not recommended with lower back conditions or if you're obese. • If pregnant, seek medical advice before attempting whip kick.

VIDEO

Freestyle

FREESTYLE		
IS IT EASY TO LEARN?	**BENEFITS**	**LIMITATIONS**
• Breathing: difficult (inhaling sideways). • Kicking**: easy (flutter kick). • Coordination: difficult (arms alternate and legs alternate).	• The fastest and most efficient stroke. • Widely perceived as the 'proper' way to swim (in Australia). • An option for people who've suffered a trauma and wish to conquer their fear of getting their face wet. • The only accepted stroke in a triathlon.	• Not recommended with a torn rotator cuff (injured shoulder).

**From my experience, *most* people can naturally flutter kick, and find learning the breaststroke whip kick challenging, particularly if you never learnt it when younger. (The whip kick is otherwise known as the frog kick.) However some people do naturally have a good ankle flex that's able to whip kick (and conversely find the flutter kick difficult). You'll soon discover which one you are as you progress through the kicking exercises later.

Although most adults wish to learn the 'proper' way, remember to modify movements based on any physical limitations you may have. Ultimately the goal is for you to discover the enjoyment that comes with swimming and be able to get from A to B safely and with ease.

Who is anyone to judge you?

7.5 HOW TO STRUCTURE YOUR PRACTICE SESSIONS

It's at this point that I'd like you to consider what kind of learner you are. Do you like to continually repeat an exercise until you master it, or do you prefer to vary your practice and build on different skills during the same session? I've taught some students who are happy to work through the same drill over and over for a whole hour, whilst others prefer to undertake a wide range of exercises on both front and back over half an hour.

Identify how you learn best to help to maximise your own productivity and motivation.

*Aim to **set a goal for every session** you undertake. It doesn't need to necessarily involve mastering a new skill, it could involve repetitions to get more comfortable in something you've just learnt how to do. Short-term goal setting should be aligned with achieving your longer-term goals, which you would've now identified from the above tables.*

It's completely okay to change your goals during your learning journey; this has happened plenty of times with my students.

8: BEGINNER BLUES

This chapter is by no means meant to discourage you in any way but rather to reassure you that these experiences are very common, particularly if you classify yourself as Swimmer A (beginner with fear) having little or no prior experience of being in a body of water.

- **Water entering your body** is the most common thing to happen to people; regardless of level. *Every* swimmer at one point or another has experienced this, particularly in the mouth. Water in the eyes and nose can sting, and water in the ears may block your hearing, causing you to feel clogged.

Refer to Chapter 6.7 'Equipment to wear' for solutions to prevent water in the eyes, nose and ears. Refer to Chapter 9.3 'Breath control' to prevent water in the mouth and nose.

TIPS

- **Feeling tightness in your chest** is due to the pressure of water against your body. Your breathing might feel restricted, until you get used to this sensation. It's normal to be sensitive to this if you're Swimmer A (beginner with fear). It's like getting used to the air pressure in your ears when you're new to flying.

If you suspect the tightness is caused by overexertion, stop your practice session immediately and seek medical advice.

ALERT

- **Feeling tired and having stiff/sore muscles**. It's very easy to underestimate how learning practical skills in the water can be both mentally and physically exhausting! Listen to your body and stop when you feel you've reached your limit. Focus on quality practice time rather than duration.

- The **smell of chlorine or the sticky feeling of salty water** on your skin and hair. There are special post-swim shampoos/conditioners and shower gels which may help.

Refer to Chapter 6.7 'Equipment to wear' for suggestions to protect your hair.

TIPS

- **Sneezing** can be your body's reaction to chemicals in the water, or if you simply have a sensitive nose. If you've a tendency to sneeze, I recommend using wet wipes rather than paper tissues because they're more robust and won't disintegrate with wet hands.

- **Dry skin** is usually caused by chlorine or salty water, as well as the heat of the sun if outdoors. Pack a bottle of a moisturising shower gel and/or lotion to rehydrate your skin afterwards.

- **Muscle cramps** can occur in the leg (calf muscle) or foot. They can be brought on through intense exercise, fatigue, mineral deficiencies, unfamiliar use of a muscle group, cold water or dehydration (it's easy to not realise you're sweating when in water!) Perhaps you've a history of cramping and know what conditions make you prone to them. For example, a student Natalie always got them when she felt nervous.

To help avoid cramping, take a bottle of water to sip during your practice (even if you think you're drinking enough water from the pool!)

TIPS

If you do experience a cramp, try to stretch the muscle and take enough rest between activities. Too much repetition can result in the overuse of a certain muscle.

- **Breathlessness** is very common and can either be due to incorrect technique or lack of stamina. You may also experience this if you hyperventilate due to nerves.

Make sure you're breathing calmly before starting any exercise.

TIPS

- **Feeling bloated and/or burping**. If you're hungry, your body can 'churn' air which can lead to feeling bloated. It can also happen if you're swallowing air and trapping gas in your stomach.

- **Feeling uncomfortable/heavy in the stomach** is most likely caused by eating too much and/or too soon before entering the water.

TIPS

Allow at least half an hour after eating for your food to settle before your practice.

- **Feeling unstable** is perfectly normal. It may take time for you to understand how your body behaves in water and to feel in control.

TIPS

Refer to Ex 9A 'Walking in water' and Chapter 10 'Floating horizontally' to get familiar and confident with controlling your body's movements.

- **Greater awareness of any physical weaknesses or imbalances.** In many ways, swimming involves symmetry. Lots of people have a clear dominant side. Others have a dominant side but play sport on their non-dominant side. For example those who are right-handed but kick a football with their left leg. You'll soon realise (if you aren't already aware) how a particular side of your body can react differently in the water and affect your balance. The key is to be aware of how a weaker side may affect your movement, so you can dedicate effort to readdress the balance. I'll cover this in more detail by stroke in Chapters 12 to 14.

NOTES

Past injuries – no matter how long ago – can also be a major influence. I couldn't understand why a student Tom had a very dominant left kick despite him insisting that he didn't have any mobility issues (and being right-handed). I later learnt that he had broken his left ankle decades earlier as a young child and undergone physiotherapy. So it can often be the area of injury that is in fact dominant and stronger following focused rehabilitation.

- **Neck strain** is a sign of tension. Try to relax and let the water support your head when horizontal. If you experience neck strain with survival breaststroke (with head permanently above water), consider reverting to competitive breaststroke instead (with head and body horizontal most of the time).

- **Lower back pain** can be due to arching your back with breaststroke or lifting your head with freestyle. Lifting your head with freestyle is incorrect, however arching the back is, to a certain extent, necessary with breaststroke.

!

ALERT

If you have a back condition my recommendation is to avoid breaststroke.

- **Feeling the need to urinate** is due to the water pressure working your kidneys (particularly in warm water). This is normal and not necessarily a sign that you've drunk lots of water from the pool! Make sure you know where the toilets are in case you need to make a visit during your practice session.

9: FUNDAMENTALS OF BEING IN WATER

Being immersed in a body of water can be a new sensation, particularly if you're Swimmer A (beginner with fear). The water's resistance makes movements much slower than on land, requiring more effort.

Your level of fear will determine the length of time and the pace you'll be able to work through this chapter. Remember to be patient with yourself.

9.1 EASY ENTRY AND EXIT. WALKING IN WATER.

 Ex 9A: Easy entry and exit. Walking in water.
EXERCISE

Training aid: or
KICKBOARD   NOODLE

Learning points:

- Identifying the shallow end of the pool (by referring to depth markers) so you can stand on the pool floor.

- Entering the pool safely using steps or a ladder.

- Submerging into a body of water and getting familiar with the water pressure against your chest.

- Getting used to the water's resistance and sense of weightlessness as the water supports you.

- Exiting the pool safely using steps or a ladder.

Entering the water via a ladder

Steps:

1. Enter the shallow end of the pool using steps or a ladder.

If the latter, hold the rails with the ladder facing you. Ensure your feet are firmly on the pool floor before moving away.

2. Walk in water at a depth that you feel comfortable, holding a kickboard or noodle with arms outstretched (see illustrations below). If you struggle with stability, a noodle is easier.

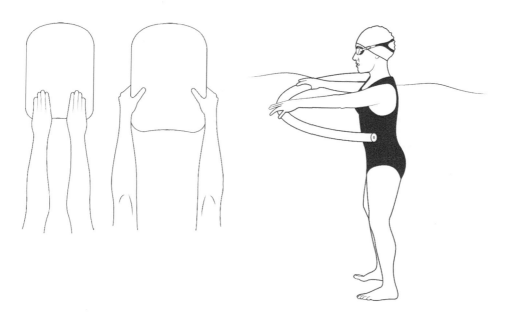

3. Exit the pool using steps or a ladder. If the latter, hold the rails with the ladder facing you.

HOME

Sit in the bath submerging your body, to get used to the water pressure against your chest.

TIPS

*Remember to **breathe**! Holding breath creates tension. Try to relax and concentrate on breathing regularly with your head permanently above the water.*

Easier alternatives:

*   Stay within arm's reach of the pool edge in case you panic.

*   Use one hand to guide yourself along the pool edge instead of holding a flotation aid.

Harder alternatives:

- Walk without holding any flotation aids.
- If pool dimensions allow, start at a very shallow depth, gradually increasing to chest or neck depth.
- Take longer strides.
- Raise your knees high.
- Walk with hands on your head or behind your neck.
- Walk sideways.
- Walk backwards.
- Scoop underwater with each hand alternately (called 'doggy paddling') to get used to the feel of the water.

9.2 DIFFICULT EXIT AND ENTRY

 ALERT *These may be impractical and/or unsafe if you're overweight, pregnant or have restricted mobility or cardiovascular problems.*

  Ex 9B: Difficult exit (climbing out of water without easy access)

VIDEO   EXERCISE

Learning points:

- Gaining confidence in exiting a body of water without easy access. For example to climb up a steep riverbank or climb back onto a surfboard.
  As a student Neil once explained; "I want to learn this so that when I go cliff diving, if a mate pushes me in, I know how to climb out easily, and be able to then push him in!"

Steps:

1. Choose a spot by the pool edge which is either at standing depth or slightly deeper (if you wish to simulate an open water scenario). Either way, ideally start with your feet off the ground to avoid cheating by jumping up from the pool floor.

2. Face the pool edge and prop your elbows onto it.

3. Push your body up high enough to be able to raise one of your knees onto the pool edge.

4. Use your knee to lever the rest of your body out of the water.

HOME

Practise from step two onwards, climbing from the floor onto a sofa or bed.

VIDEO

EXERCISE

Ex 9C: Difficult entry (sliding into water without easy access)

Learning points:

• Gaining confidence in entering a body of water without easy access.

For example to enter a river from the bank or to enter the ocean from a boat without a ladder.

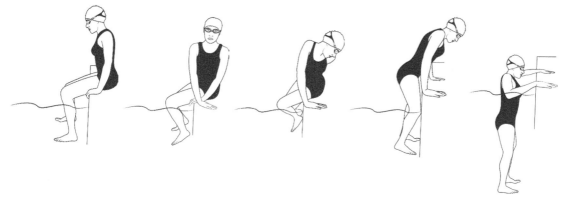

Steps:

1. Sit on the pool edge with legs submerged, *where you know it's at standing depth.*

2. Place both hands firmly on one side of your body.

3.   Turn your body around so you've rolled onto your stomach and your back faces the water.

4.   Lower your body gradually into the water feet first, taking your weight onto your hands and keeping hold of the pool edge at all times.

ALERT

It's important to get into the habit of entering water with your back to it. ***Don't descend facing the water (as illustrated below).***

How not to enter the water: risk of slippage

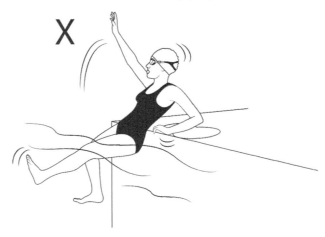

If the surface is wet, you could lose control of your descent causing your head and body to tip backwards and risking injury. You'll be able to maintain a tighter grip on land when facing towards it, which is particularly important when entering open water with possible undercurrents.

HOME

Practise from step 2 onwards, sliding to the floor from a seated position on a sofa or bed.

9.3 BREATH CONTROL

Breath control is the most common issue that adults face – and the most fundamental skill to get right.

It's absolutely crucial in order to master water confidence.

People often report "I can't get enough air" or "I catch water in my mouth" or comment "Swimming would be so much easier if I didn't have to breathe!".

Holding your breath is unfortunately very common. But if you don't exhale, how will you have the lung capacity to inhale? Breath holding creates tension that leads to breathlessness and fatigue. Hyperventilating is the opposite extreme. This can also cause breathlessness and can lead to dizziness. Either way, you won't be able to establish a comfortable rhythm to sustain swimming for long.

The general rule of thumb is to ensure there's always a *constant airflow*; inhaling above water, exhaling underwater, and controlling the volumes of both. The sounds and sights of bubbles moving past your face may be new to you and something to get used to, particularly if you're previously used to holding your breath. As a student Mary remarked, "It's about realising they are *my* bubbles!"

THE CORRECT BREATHING TECHNIQUE WHILST SWIMMING IS:

- **INHALE THROUGH MOUTH** *ONLY:* **ABOVE WATER.**
- **EXHALE THROUGH MOUTH AND NOSE** *TOGETHER:* **BELOW WATER.**

Getting proficient with the above can be challenging, as it's not a skill you would usually perform on land. It can be particularly tricky if you're experienced in meditation, yoga, pilates or scuba diving. This is because these practices involve both a different method to breathe as well as a different speed in which to do it in.

TIPS

- *Try to think of it as continuously exhaling unless inhaling.*
- *Don't open your mouth too wide otherwise you could catch water when you inhale, and exhale too fast. Think of a small whistle-shaped mouth, or blowing through a straw.*
- *It's about exhaling strong enough to stop water going in, but not too strong that you need to inhale very often.*
- *Focus on slow, deep breaths in and out. (You can work towards more natural breathing, like you'd do on land, once you feel more comfortable.)*

Generally speaking, the students I've taught wish to learn the correct way to breathe whilst swimming. However there are some who are able to breathe differently without any side-effects of water entering their body. My philosophy is that if it ain't broke, don't fix it. Ultimately what's important is to feel comfortable in water.

The two alternative breathing techniques whilst swimming are:

1. Inhale through mouth *only*: above water.

   Exhale through mouth *only*: below water.

NOTES

- *If you're a natural mouth breather, you may find this method the easiest to grasp.*
- *Don't cheat by pinching your nose shut with one hand – you'll ultimately need both your hands to move in the water!*

TIPS

Consider wearing nose clips if you wish to adopt this breathing technique but find water enters your nose. 'Refer to Chapter 6.7 'Equipment to wear' for more information.

2. Inhale through mouth *only*: above water.

   Exhale through nose *only*: below water (with mouth closed).

The following exercises are based on mastering the correct breath control technique.

  Ex 9D: Mouth bubbles at the surface

VIDEO   EXERCISE

Learning points:

- How to blow slow, continuous and relaxed bubbles.

- Getting used to the sights and sounds of bubbles near the face. It should start to feel and sound relaxing once you get used to it.

- How to stop water from entering the mouth.

- Knowing when to ascend in order to inhale *before* your lungs are empty. You don't wait until completely out of air before inhaling when running or cycling – why would you do so here?!

- How to inhale from your belly rather than the top of your lungs (to avoid hyperventilating). In other words, breathing in from your lower chest not upper chest.

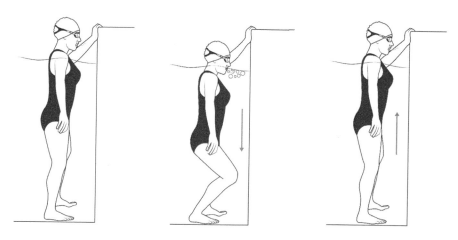

Steps:

1. Stand with your feet flat on the pool floor. Relax.
2. Inhale through mouth.
3. Bend your knees and keep your head looking forward.
4. Exhale through *mouth only* at the water's surface. There should be a *continuous* stream of bubbles coming from your mouth.
5. Stand up to inhale through your mouth, once you've exhaled *most* of your air. Don't wait until your lungs have completely emptied otherwise you'll panic and be gasping!

PROBLEM	REASON	SOLUTION
You're exhaling sporadically in sharp bursts.	You're not used to blowing bubbles.	Try humming to ensure a steady and continuous flow of bubbles.
You can't exhale.	You're holding your breath which is a sign of tension and fear that you'll run out of air.	Try humming to ensure a steady and continuous flow of bubbles. Start exhaling *as you descend*.
You're getting water in your nose.	You've descended too low.	Only submerge low enough for your mouth to be at the water's surface. Imagine you're cooling a hot drink.
You're catching water in your mouth on your descent.	You didn't start to exhale soon enough.	Remember to exhale *all the time* whenever you're not inhaling. Start exhaling *as you descend*.
You're catching water in your mouth on your ascent.	You're opening your mouth too soon to inhale.	Either slow down your exhalation (so you need to inhale later) or ascend sooner to inhale.

Hold the pool edge for support when bending your knees.

VIDEO

EXERCISE

Ex 9E: Mouth and nose bubbles underwater

Learning points:

- How to blow bubbles from both mouth and nose *together*. This is a new skill that you wouldn't have tried before – it's not something we'd ever do on land!

- Deciding if you wish to wear nose clips (if you can't exhale from both mouth and nose together and find water entering your nose).

- Submerging low enough to wet your goggles and getting used to keeping your eyes open.

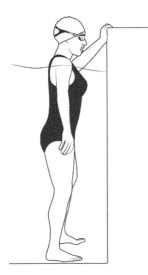

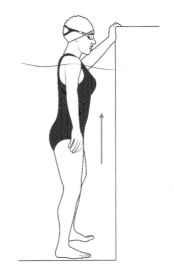

Steps:

1. Repeat Ex 9D, descending a little deeper so that your nose is submerged as well as your mouth.

   Blow nose bubbles as well as mouth bubbles at step 4.

PROBLEM	REASON	SOLUTION
You're alternating between exhaling from mouth then nose.	You're not used to blowing bubbles through both mouth and nose together. This is common.	Keep practising! Or consider getting nose clips.
You're catching water in the nose.	You're not exhaling long or strong enough from the nose (it tends to be easier to blow mouth bubbles rather than nose bubbles).	Practice exhaling through nose *only*, then gradually add exhaling through mouth so that you're doing it together.
	You may be inhaling from the nose.	Imagine you have a cold and your nose is blocked. Focus on inhaling only from the mouth.

VIDEO

EXERCISE

Ex 9F: Breathing in and out

Learning points:

- Getting confident with a continuous airflow of *one single breath in* and *one single breath out.*

- Getting your whole face wet (looking down to the pool floor rather than forwards).

- Deciding whether to wear ear plugs or a cap to seal the ears (if you can't get used to water entering your ears).

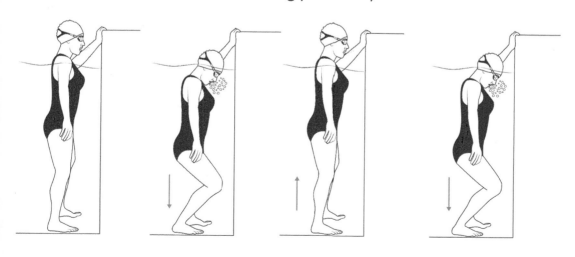

Steps:

1. Repeat Ex 9E, bobbing up and down with feet remaining firmly on the pool floor. Inhale through mouth above the water and bend your knees to exhale through mouth and nose underwater, looking downwards.

NOTES

Don't pause between submersions to breathe in and out a few times! Focus on one single breath in and one single breath out.

TIPS

- *Tuck your chin in to look downwards so that the water level sits at the crown of your head (or the rim of your swim cap).*

HOME

- *Practise in a sink or a bath.*

Easier alternative:

- Guide yourself down to submerge using the rungs of a ladder.

Harder alternative:

- Submerge deeper by trying to touch your knees or toes, or retrieve an object from various depths. This trains you to ration out your bubbles so you don't run out of air.

  It also tests whether you're keeping your eyes open, as otherwise you can't see what you're doing underwater.

  You'll also get a sense of your own natural buoyancy because the water will start to push you upwards as you descend.

PROBLEM	REASON	SOLUTION
You're running out of air.	You're waiting too long to ascend to inhale.	Ascend once you've expelled most of your air but *before* you need to inhale.
	You're rushing the inhale. You may feel more comfortable with your face down than up.	Inhale slower (remember you're in control with your feet firmly on the pool floor).
	You're rushing the exhale. You may feel more comfortable with your face up than down.	Exhale slower (this will help to avoid panic). Get used to seeing and hearing your bubbles pass your face. Ensure you do it with a whistle-shaped mouth to control the volume expelled.
You can't inhale.	You haven't exhaled enough to have the lung capacity to take in air.	Focus on a longer or stronger exhalation.
	You're rushing the inhale. This is common when you feel more comfortable face down than up.	Relax! You're in control with your feet firmly on the pool floor.
You're not getting enough air.	You're delaying your inhale due to fear of catching water. It's a sign of lack of confidence.	Practise will help you to build confidence in opening your mouth sooner to allow more time to breathe in.
You're closing your eyes automatically when looking down.	You may be used to wearing leaking goggles and instinctively now close your eyes. Or you may not feel comfortable with your face down and bubbles passing your face.

It's very important to get into the habit of keeping your eyes open. | Look at your feet when exhaling or practise picking up something from the bottom of the pool. It'll force you to keep your eyes open when submerged. |

9.4 BREATHING AND WALKING IN WATER

  Ex 9G: Breathing and walking in water

VIDEO   EXERCISE

Training aid: or

KICKBOARD   NOODLE

Learning points:

- Multi-tasking walking in water (Ex 9A) together with breathing in and out (Ex 9F).

Steps:

1. Repeat Ex 9F while walking in water holding a noodle or a kickboard with arms outstretched (see illustrations below). Bend your knees and look at your feet when exhaling.

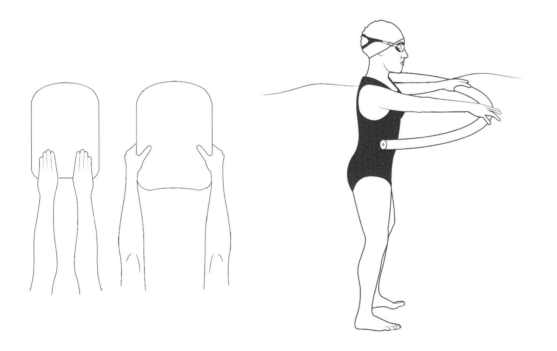

PROBLEM	REASON	SOLUTION
My legs keep floating up!	You're leaning forward rather than bending your knees.	Squat and look at your feet as you walk or find a shallower depth so you can maintain your balance better.
You can't breathe and walk at the same time.	You're finding it difficult to multi-task.	Develop a pattern of a certain number of steps to inhale and exhale with, to create a rhythm to your breathing and help you to coordinate. For example, exhale facing down for two steps forward, inhale facing up for one step forward.
You keep wiping water away from your face.	You're not used to the side-effect of water running down your face.	Resist the temptation to wipe your face after every ascent! You won't have your hands free to do this when you're ultimately swimming. *Get used to this by breathing under a running shower at home.*

Easier alternative:

- Exhale looking forwards rather than downwards.

10: FLOATING HORIZONTALLY

10.1 Reasons why horizontal floating is important

10.2 Five factors that influence the ability and length of a float

10.3 Linking front and back floats

10.1 REASONS WHY HORIZONTAL FLOATING IS IMPORTANT

It teaches you:

- How to be horizontal.

  As humans we spend most of our waking hours in vertical positions. Swimming involves getting familiar with being horizontal.

- How to trust the water.

  Knowing the water can support your body and stopping the instinctive need to move excessively. *You shouldn't be moving forwards or backwards.*

- Awareness of your own buoyancy.

  Where you lie naturally when the water is pushing your body upwards.

- How to rotate your body.

  Controlling your movements and balance in the water through transitioning from vertical to horizontal and then back to a stable standing position.

- Breath control (when front floating).

  Awareness of your own lung capacity to manage the volume of air by exhaling slowly and continuously, without rushing.

TIPS

If you're Swimmer A (beginner with fear) try to get into the habit of practising a front float at the start of every session, even if you prefer to ultimately only develop back swimming skills. This will give you the confidence to know how to relax and breathe if your face gets wet.

Many adults are convinced they can't float. Indeed, it's very common to not be able to sustain a *motionless* float; you may find you'll need to move a little to stop your body from dropping too fast. However kicking a lot is generally a sign of lack of trust in the water to support you. It's what I observe from students who've attended classes that skipped straight into teaching strokes without covering the fundamentals of floating first.

10.2 FIVE FACTORS THAT INFLUENCE THE ABILITY AND LENGTH OF A FLOAT

1. **Water type.** Salty water boosts buoyancy, helping you to float higher and for longer.

2. **Your bone and muscle density.** Fat floats and muscle sinks. That means if you're muscular, thin or lean, it'll be more difficult for you to float. Older adults may find floating easier as their bone density has reduced. If you have an asymmetric body (that is, you're not evenly proportioned) this will affect your density and therefore balance in the water. For example, if you've more muscles in one arm than the other due to playing a racquet sport, or you've had a hip replacement.

3. **Your level of confidence.** If you're tense, muscles contract and become heavier, causing you to sink quicker – so try to relax!

4. **The air in your lungs.** Air in your body boosts buoyancy. That's why generally your upper body can be higher than your lower body due to the air in your lungs and weight of muscle developed in your legs. Back floating exemplifies this because the body rises slightly when inhaling and falls slightly when exhaling.

5. **Clothing type and style.** The neoprene material in a wetsuit boosts buoyancy, helping you to float higher and for longer. A student Sarah had a zip in the front of her swimming costume which she used to tuck in a mini kickboard and thereby was able to float much easier!

Ex 10A: Front float and standing up (vertical rotation)

Learning points:

*   Understanding your body's natural buoyancy in water.

*   How to exhale slowly and be aware of when to stand up *before* the need to inhale.

*   How to stand up from being horizontal.

Getting onto a front float

Steps:

1. Lay your hands on the water's surface with arms outstretched.

2. Inhale looking forward and bend your knees to exhale face down.

3. Lean forward to allow your legs to float up. Your head determines the rest of your body position, and your body operates on a pivot. So tuck your chin in to raise your legs.

*   *Always prioritise your breathing before moving the rest of your body. If you can't control your breathing, you'll panic.*
*   *Having your legs apart will spread out your weight and help to balance in the water.*

TIPS

PROBLEM	REASON	SOLUTION
You're moving forward.	You're leaping forward.	Don't launch onto your front; bend your knees, exhale face down and pull up your hips gradually.
You're sinking.	Your face is looking forward rather than downward. This will cause your legs to drop. It's a sign of lack of confidence as you're worried about not being able to inhale after the float or fear falling forward.	Tuck your chin in so that your ears are between your shoulders. This will help to raise your legs.
	Your legs are causing you to sink.	Try moving your arms closer towards your ears to counteract your leg weight.

VIDEO

Front float to standing

NOTES

The recovery can arguably be more of a concern than the float itself. I often find students so preoccupied with getting back to their feet that they rush the float. This is normal!

Steps:

The following points should all be done *at the same time.*

1. Bend your knees towards your chest, as if to sit.

2. Lean backwards and look forwards (remember your head determines the rest of your body position, so looking forwards will help your legs to drop).

3. Use your arms to *push the water down and back* with your hands in a long sweeping motion.

NOTES

It doesn't matter whether you place one foot down and then the other, or both feet together. The most important thing is the end result: standing.

PROBLEM	REASON	SOLUTION
You're rushing to stand or finding it's taking too long.	The recovery is not instantaneous! Many people panic when it doesn't happen quickly. Remember the water's resistance means any movement *takes time*.	Think of doing it in slow motion and exhale slowly to allow yourself plenty of time to stand without running out of air.
You're catching water when trying to inhale.	You may be closing your eyes whilst underwater.	Keep your eyes open to know when you're clear of the water to inhale.
	You may not be exhaling long or strong enough.	Focus on exhaling *continuously* until you're clear of the water.

Easier alternatives:

- Practise the float in very shallow water, like a paddling pool or spa (if there's room).

- If you're struggling with the confidence to lift your feet from the pool floor, practise bunny hops to get used to the movement.

- If you fear falling forwards or are anxious about standing, hold onto a step or ladder (the pool edge may not allow you to get completely horizontal).

You can then transition to holding a noodle with arms outstretched – which is still something solid to hold onto – but less fixed of course. Some of my nervous students find pushing the noodle up against the wall helps. Try to hold the noodle lightly with fingertips rather than your whole hands; it's otherwise difficult to let go and transition to an independent float!

Ex 10B: Back float and standing up (vertical rotation)
EXERCISE

Learning points:

- Understanding your body's natural buoyancy in water.

- How to stand up from being horizontal.

Getting onto a back float
VIDEO

The good news is that you can breathe easy on your back since you're facing up! So that's one thing less to have to concentrate on.

Steps:

1. Lay your hands on the surface of the water with arms outstretched behind you and palms facing up.

2. Bend your knees to lower your body in the water so that your ears are wet and you're facing up.

3. Gently pull up your hips to allow your legs to float up. Your head determines the rest of your body position, and your body operates on a pivot. So lift your chin up to raise your legs.

Having your legs apart will spread out your weight and help to balance in the water.

TIPS

PROBLEM	REASON	SOLUTION
You're moving backward and submerging.	You're leaping backward.	Don't launch onto your back; bend your knees, look up and pull up your hips gradually.
You're sinking.	Your face is looking forward rather than upward. This will cause your legs to drop. It's a sign of lack of confidence as you're worried about getting back to your feet or fear falling backwards.	Lift your chin up so that your ears are wet. This will help to raise your legs.
	Your legs are causing you to sink.	Try moving your arms closer towards your ears to counteract your leg weight.
You're losing your balance.	You may be closing your eyes.	Keep your eyes open to give you confidence of knowing where you are.

VIDEO

Back float to standing

NOTES

The recovery can arguably be more of a concern than the float itself. I often find students so preoccupied with getting back to their feet that they rush the float. This is normal!

Steps:

The following points should all be done *at the same time.*

1. Bend your knees towards your chest, as if to sit.

2. Lean forwards and look forward tucking in chin (remember your head determines the rest of your body position, so looking forward will help your legs to drop).

3. Use your arms to *scoop the water up* with your hands in a long sweeping motion.

NOTES

It doesn't matter whether you place one foot down and then the other, or both feet together. The most important thing is the end result: standing.

PROBLEM	REASON	SOLUTION
You're rushing to stand or finding it's taking too long.	The recovery is not instantaneous! Many people panic when it doesn't happen quickly. Remember the water's resistance means any movement *takes time*.	Think of doing it in slow motion.
You're tipping to the side whilst standing up.	Your head isn't centred as you roll forward.	Practise leaning forward and blow bubbles face down, so you roll your head forward, as if to bow.
You can't find your feet easily.	You may be trying to avoid getting your face wet for fear of catching water.	Inhale whilst on your back and exhale as you roll forward. That way if your face gets wet, you won't panic as water can't get in.

Easier alternatives:

- If you fear falling backwards or are anxious about standing, lean onto a step (the pool edge may not allow you to get completely horizontal). Try floating briefly by yourself (hovering your body above the step). You can start by resting your elbows on the step, then progressively work until just your fingertips are supporting you with arms extended.

- NOODLE KICKBOARD Use a noodle across your back and hold it with both hands, which is still something solid to hold onto – but less fixed of course.

Then try moving your arms away from the noodle so your legs and arms are in a star shaped position. Some of my nervous students find leaning with the noodle up against the wall helps. Focus on getting your ears wet.

- Hold a pair of kickboards or a pair of noodles (as illustrated below) and slowly transition away from them. Note that if you let go of only one flotation aid on your back, you're likely to lose balance. Make sure you focus on loosening your hand grip on both sides *simultaneously*. Try to hold the noodles lightly with fingertips rather than your whole hands; it's otherwise difficult to let go and transition to an independent float!

Back float holding two noodles (view from above)

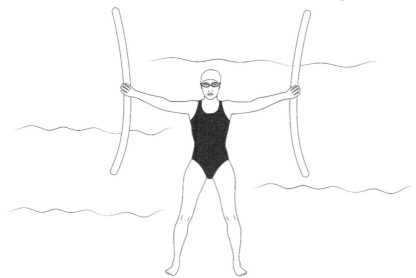

10.3 LINKING FRONT AND BACK FLOATS

Being proficient at rotating between front and back floats is important; particularly in the direction *from* front *to* back. This is a key survival skill because you'll know how to flip onto your back should you ever panic or get tired on your front.

There are two ways to do this:

1. Turning sideways (horizontal rotation).

2. Turning lengthways (vertical rotation).

You would've mastered turning lengthways to some extent when learning how to stand from a horizontal float, as explained in Ex 10A and Ex 10B. Turning sideways is quicker as the axis to do so is very short and offers less resistance. This is therefore the easier rotation to master.

VIDEO   EXERCISE

Ex 10C: From front float to back float (horizontal rotation)

Learning points:

- How to rotate your body horizontally from front to back, in case you get tired or panic on your front. This is a key survival skill.

- Exhaling until your face is completely clear.

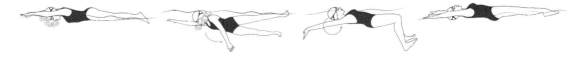

Steps:

1. Once you're front floating, drop the arm of the side you plan to turn towards and turn your head to face up. The rest of your body will follow.

2. Continue to exhale through both mouth *and nose* until your face is clear of the water.

TIPS

- *An alternative way to consider this movement is: pull with your opposite arm (of your turning direction) to flip onto your back.*
- *It doesn't matter which direction you choose to rotate.*
- *Remember to exhale from your nose as well as mouth! (This is often forgotten.)*

PROBLEM	REASON	SOLUTION
You find yourself standing.	You're looking forward as you turn, causing your legs to drop. Remember your head determines the rest of your body position.	Visualise the back float and *look up* as you roll, keeping your chin up.
You're getting water in mouth and/or nose.	You're not exhaling strong or long enough.	Keep exhaling until your face is clear on your back. Remember to wear your nose clip if you usually wear this on your back.
You can't seem to turn over onto your back.	You're not rolling your head and looking up.	Practise to develop your confidence in turning your head. Visualise the back float.
	You haven't dropped one arm to your side (it's impossible to turn if you stay star-shaped).	Drop the arm of the side you plan to turn towards.

Easier alternative:

- Practise the easier direction which is from a *back* float to a *front* float. The same rule applies; drop the arm of the side you plan to turn towards. Remember to start to exhale before rolling onto your front with face down.

11: FLOATING VERTICALLY (TREADING WATER)

11.1 DEFINITION OF TREADING WATER

Treading water is a float whereby you're able to keep your head – or more specifically your mouth – above the water level in depths where you can't stand. *It's (incorrectly) referred to by some people as 'threading water'.*

NOTES

Treading water is typically a fully vertical float, however it can also be done with your lower body horizontal (as illustrated on the following page). This can be to prevent your legs becoming tangled with underwater hazards like water weeds, and demands more upper body strength.

Treading water to avoid underwater hazards

11.2 REASONS WHY TREADING WATER IS IMPORTANT

I never cease to be amazed at how often it's neglected to be taught in adult swim classes; even though it's a very important survival skill. Many people I've met can swim over deep water – or are very experienced in water sports on top of the water – but don't know how to tread water. Students often remark that people seem to do it so effortlessly – and wonder what on earth is going on underneath the water that helps to prop their body up!

Advantages of being able to tread water:

- To give you **independence to swim at any depth** without the fear of drowning.

- To be able to stop swimming and **look around** in areas that you can't stand.

- To be able to **talk with others** in deep water.

- To be able to **signal to others** in deep water in the event of an emergency.

A student Richard reported that in his previous adult classes he was asked to simply jump into the deep end and tread water to return to the pool edge, without any detailed instructions on exactly how to do so. Treading water is not something that necessarily comes instinctively. I'll break down the skill step by step below.

TIPS

Treading water is a tiring and difficult skill to learn – more so than people realise. Practise a little but often (so you don't get frustrated). You can then work on gradually extending the time you can do it for.

NOTES

The length of time that you should be able to tread for depends on where you swim. If you wish to swim only in a pool, then five seconds may be sufficient. That's long enough to give you the confidence to swim in the deep end, and also not to panic if you get stuck behind slower swimmers in your lane! If you wish to swim in open water, then five minutes would be more realistic in the event that you're waiting for a boat to pick you up.

EXERCISE

Ex 11A: Kicking

Training aid: **or x2**

NOODLE   KICKBOARD

Learning points:

- How to kick in a vertical position with legs underneath your body.
- Identifying which type of kick(s) you wish to practise ongoing.

NOTES

It's not imperative to learn all of the different kicks but mastering at least two means you'll have an alternative kick in case you get tired doing the same one kick.

TIPS

Avoid holding onto the pool edge or ladder, as you'll naturally navigate towards the pool edge. This will restrict your space and ability to kick.

Steps:

1. Prop your body up with a noodle either around your back, across your chest or holding two kickboards on either side of your body. This will give space for your legs to move without hitting your feet on the pool floor at standing depth. Hold the noodle or two kickboards with both hands for balance. Keep your body upright as this is a *vertical* float.

2. VIDEO Try the **bicycle kick with a noodle**.

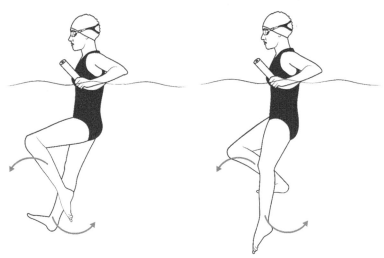

Use the soles of your feet to push the water down, like pedalling an imaginary bicycle underwater. Your legs can either be close together or wide apart (for balance).

This can be straightforward if you already developed muscle memory as a kid of riding a bicycle (if not, see tip below!)

NOTES

It doesn't matter which direction you pedal, although most people tend to pedal forwards. If you do so, focus on kicking your bottom with your heels.

TIPS

If you never learnt how to ride a bicycle, consider riding the spinning bike at the gym to build muscle memory in the leg movements.

3. Try the **scissor kick with a noodle**.

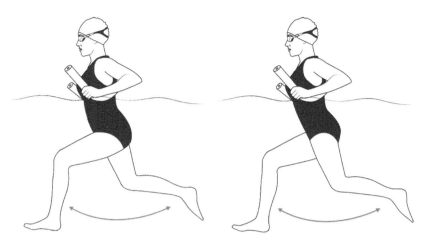

Move your legs backwards and forwards in an alternating continuous action from your hips, like a pendulum. You should have floppy feet and loose ankles. Depending on the depth of water, you may need to bend your knees to avoid hitting your feet on the pool floor. This is fine so long as you still kick from your *hips* and not from your *knees*.

Correcting a rushed scissor kick

If your scissor kick feels rushed, you may not be moving your knees as far behind your body as in front of it. Start with one foot in front and the other behind, then get faster until your legs are suspended above the pool floor.

NOTES

- *It should be a slow movement compared with the bicycle kick. This is because you're using the whole surface area of your legs to push through the water's resistance compared to just the soles of your feet with the bicycle kick.*

TIPS

- *If you've already mastered a flutter kick from Chapter 12 'Backstroke' or Chapter 14 'Freestyle', consider this as a slower and larger version of it, performed vertically rather than horizontally.*

🎥 Try the egg beater kick with a noodle
VIDEO

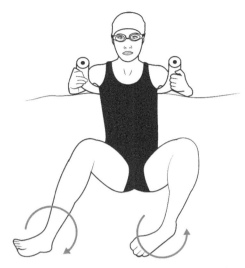

Raise your knees high enough to draw circles with your feet in opposite directions.

Your hips should move from side to side with mainly your lower legs moving with floppy feet and loose ankles.

NOTES

- *It's normal to have a better circular kick with your dominant leg. It'll simply take some practice for your non-dominant leg to get stronger and more proficient.*
- *If you're turning around in the water, it's likely that both feet are (incorrectly) circling in the same direction rather than opposite directions, or that you have a strong dominant leg.*

TIPS

- *If your feet are hitting each other, circle your feet alternately rather than simultaneously.*
- *Think of the movement as circling clockwise with one foot and anti-clockwise with the other foot.*
- *Think of the movement as both feet circling in an inward direction or both feet circling in an outward direction. (You may find it more natural for your feet to circle in one particular direction. There's no right or wrong; identify which direction feels easier for you.)*

HOME

- *Practise this kick sitting on a chair (on land) to build muscle memory in the movement.*

PROBLEM	REASON	SOLUTION
Your legs are coming in front of your body.	You're most likely leaning backwards.	Make sure your legs stay underneath and your torso remains upright.
Your legs are behind your body.	You're most likely leaning forwards.	Make sure your legs stay underneath and your torso remains upright.

TIPS

- *If you can already do the breaststroke whip kick, you could try this instead of the kicks suggested above. Note however that there's a moment in between each breaststroke kick when your legs aren't pushing your body upwards; so you'll find yourself bobbing up and down. It can therefore be a little harder to keep yourself sustained above the water level.*

VIDEO   EXERCISE

Ex 11B: Sculling

Learning points:

- Discovering the correct angle, range and power for you to move your hands and arms in order to raise your body up. (This differs from person to person and ultimately depends on your own body density.)

- Working out whether to move both arms together or alternating (there's no right or wrong).

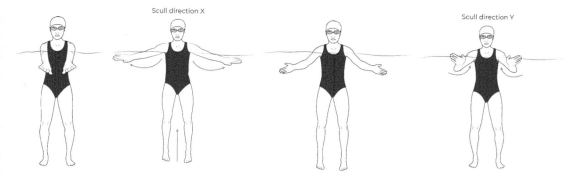

Steps:

1. Stand with your feet flat on the ground.

2. Sweep arms apart, palms facing outwards with thumbs down. This is scull direction X. (It's similar to Ex 13D 'Breaststroke arms'.) Then sweep arms together, palms facing inwards with thumbs up. This is scull direction Y. (It's similar to hands clapping together.)

Basically, you're moving your arms underwater from side to side to raise your body onto your toes. Focus on feeling an *uplift of your body.*

TIPS

- *Keep your hands and arms underwater to maximise the effectiveness of sculling. Any splashing signifies wasted energy through movements above water.*

NOTES

- *It's important to know how to scull staying in the same spot. Perhaps you're stuck in a queue behind swimmers in the same lane as you, or you're in the water chatting with friends.*

In order to do this, sculls X and Y must have the same power. That means applying equal pressure against the water for both the outward and inward sweeps.

EXERCISE

Ex 11C: Combining kicking and sculling together: treading water

Training aid:

NOODLE

Learning points:

- Multi-tasking kicking and sculling together.

NOTES

- *The sculling technique is the same regardless of the kick used.*
- *There's no set coordination between sculling and kicking; so long as your whole body is moving constantly.*

Steps:

1. Prop your body up with a noodle around your back or across your chest. This will give space for your legs to move without hitting your feet on the pool floor.

2. Practise your chosen kick together with the sculling.

PROBLEM	REASON	SOLUTION
You're moving forward.	Scull X is stronger than scull Y.	Scull in both directions with equal power.
You're moving backward.	Scull Y is stronger than scull X.	Scull in both directions with equal power.

PROBLEM	REASON	SOLUTION
You're tilted forward.	You're leaning forward.	Place the noodle around your back, to keep your body upright and legs underneath.
You're tilted backward.	You're leaning backward.	Place the noodle across your chest, keeping your body upright and legs underneath.

VIDEO   EXERCISE

Ex 11D: Treading water independently in shallow water

Learning points:

- Working out how hard to scull and kick to keep you afloat without any flotation aids.

NOTES

- *You don't need to work on raising your body any higher than having your mouth above water level, so you can breathe clearly.*

TIPS

- *Moving only your arms or only your legs (without flotation aids) is in fact a much more difficult exercise! (It can be certainly done at a more advanced level.) As a beginner, kick and scull together when practising treading water independently.*

Steps:

1. Go to a depth where you can ideally only just touch the pool floor with your feet. Face the pool edge or ladder and practise bouncing off the pool floor (exhaling when submerged) to get used to the depth.

2. Once familiar with the depth, inhale then exhale slowly and practise sculling and kicking together.

NOTES

- *The reason for exhaling slowly is twofold. Firstly, to release any tension. Remember it's important to try to relax. If you're tense, your muscles will contract and make your body heavier in the water – thereby making treading harder to achieve. Secondly, to avoid the fear of drowning as you'll block any water from entering your body if you submerge.*

Easier alternatives:

- Practise in shallower water where you can stand more easily.

- Practise in salty water to boost your buoyancy.

- Wear a snorkel (refer to Chapter 6.8 'Equipment to use') to eliminate the fear of water entering mouth or nose.

Ex 11E: Treading water independently in deeper water

EXERCISE

! *Try this only when you feel competent enough. If you feel anxious or nervous, continue practising Ex 11D or take a buddy with you for support.*

ALERT

Learning points:

- Increasing your confidence and stamina when out of depth.

- Understanding how hard to scull and kick to keep you afloat.

- As you get experienced, fine tuning *how slow* you can scull and kick and still be able to keep afloat.

Steps:

1. Repeat Ex 11D at a slightly deeper depth, still keeping the pool edge or ladder within arm's reach.

PROBLEM	REASON	SOLUTION
You can't tread for long.	Lack of stamina.	Track the length of time you can tread for and aim to extend it.
	You're holding your breath.	Remember to breathe! It'll not only extend your time but also help you to lose tension.
You're tilted backward.	You're looking up to avoid getting your face wet in fear of swallowing water.	Ensure you're looking forwards, and exhale if your head submerges.
You're tilted forward.	You're looking down.	Ensure you're looking forwards, and only exhale if your head submerges. Focus on the goal of raising your mouth above the water level.

Harder alternatives:

- Tread water without wearing goggles; it'll make your body work harder in order to prevent your face from submerging.

- If the pool floor has a sharp drop, step off the slope to start treading immediately in the deep. You'll tread harder than if you tread where you're able to always stand on tip-toes. Remember to keep either the pool edge or ladder within arm's reach.

VIDEO   EXERCISE

Ex 11F: From treading water to back float

Learning points:

- Transitioning from treading in a vertical position to being horizontal on your back, without touching the pool floor at any point. A key survival skill to understand what to do if/when you get tired treading and can't easily reach a point of safety. You can rest and recover your breathing whilst back floating.

NOTES

- *The video and illustration show the bicycle kick, however any kick described in Ex 11A can be used for this exercise.*

Steps:

1. Tread water a little first (it doesn't matter for how long).

2. Look up, kick and paddle to rotate your body into a horizontal position on your back.

TIPS

- *The key is to visualize a back float and look upward.*

Easier alternatives:

- Recap back floating (refer to Ex 10B 'Back float') from a standing position in shallow water.

- Do this exercise in reverse; start with a back float and then kick and paddle, leaning forward to transition to treading water without touching the pool floor at any point.

  Ex 11G: Treading water forwards and backwards

VIDEO   EXERCISE

Learning points:

- Understanding how to move around whilst treading water.

For example to reach a point of safety in order to climb out of deep water.

Steps:

1. To move *forwards*, scull X must be stronger than scull Y i.e. focus on sweeping hands and arms *outward*.

2. To move *backwards*, scull Y must be stronger than scull X i.e. focus on sweeping hands and arms *inward*.

- *Refer to Ex 11B for sculling techniques X and Y.*
- *Refer to Ex 15.2 for linking between treading water and a stroke.*

TIPS

12: BACKSTROKE

12.1 OVERVIEW OF BACKSTROKE IN GENERAL

Swimming on your back can often be the first way of swimming that people master; particularly if you're Swimmer A (beginner with fear). This is because you can breathe freely facing up and coordination between arms, legs and breathing isn't essential in order to move.

12.2 OVERVIEW OF 'COMPETITIVE' BACKSTROKE

BREATHING:	as you wish (establish a comfortable rhythm with your strokes).
ARMS:	continuous alternating stroke (majority of propulsion).
LEGS:	continuous alternating flutter kick (little propulsion).
PREREQUISITE:	be able to back float and stand up independently.

VIDEO   EXERCISE

Ex 12A: Flutter kick on back with kickboard

Training aid:
KICKBOARD

Learning points:

- Understanding which direction to face before starting to move on your back. (Your back should face the direction of travel.)

- How to flutter kick on your back in a horizontal, streamlined position and get used to a rocking of the hips.

- Understanding how your head directly affects your hips and leg positioning. (Lifting your head causes hips and legs to drop.)

- Getting used to no vision in the direction of travel. (Use landmarks instead as an indicator of your movement).

TIPS

Think of the flutter kick like a butterfly flutters its wings; small and fast.

NOTES

You may find that you have a different style (movement/speed) of flutter kick on your back compared with your front. This is common and will simply require practise to bring consistency on both sides.

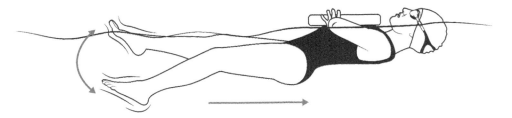

Steps:

1. Stand with your *back* facing the direction of travel.

2. Hold the board against your chest with hands on the sides and elbows stuck out. This will give you the most balance, compared with hugging the board (which will induce rolling around). Remember you can breathe as you wish.

3. Back float. Pull hips up to meet the kickboard (otherwise your body bows). Keep head still and centred.

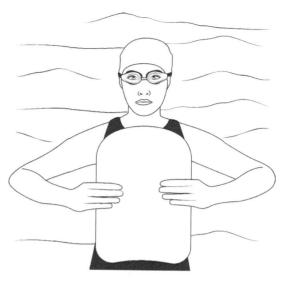

4. Bring legs together in a streamlined position and start kicking up and down in an alternating continuous action from your hips (not knees), ideally splashing your toes at the water's surface. Your knees should bend slightly with loose ankles and feet.

5. When ready to stop, let go of board *before* leaning forward so you can stand up without the board obstructing you.

Problem	Reason	Solution
You're not moving.	You're bending your knees excessively (using calf muscles rather than thigh muscles). This is called a bicycle kick (as illustrated in Ex 14A).	Kick from the hips and point your toes to straighten your legs. Think of flicking your feet rather than pedalling. **VIDEO** Lower the board so it's against your thighs (rather than across your chest). This way you can be aware of knees bending and hitting the board. The only way to move is with your feet. **FINS** A pair of short blade fins can help to straighten your legs, however you'll need to practise getting used to wearing them first and standing with them from a back float.
	You're not bending your knees enough. Your legs are too stiff.	Try to relax and bend your knees a little.

Problem	Reason	Solution
You're not moving (*cont.*)	Your legs are too low. Either you started too early (before your legs had reached their highest float) or you waited too long to start kicking (your legs started to drop after floating).	Bring legs together and start kicking when they're at their highest position in the float.
	You have a weak or big kick.	Kick fast and small.
	You're watching your feet and your body is bowing.	Look up with ears submerged. Raising your chin will raise your hips and legs and ensure your body is more horizontal.
	Your hips have dropped.	Pull up your hips towards the kickboard, so that your body straightens and becomes more horizontal. Raise your chin (so ears are submerged) to raise your legs.
	Your legs are far apart.	Kick with your legs together; a streamlined position is important to minimise resistance in the water.
	Your legs are kicking sideways.	Kick up and down.
	Your ankles are stiff/flexed with toes curled up. This is common if you're an experienced runner or cyclist.	Kick with loose ankles and feet, pointing your toes. FINS — A pair of short blade fins can help to loosen your ankles, however you'll need to practise getting used to wearing them first and standing with them from a back float.
You're getting water in your mouth and/or nose.	You're tipping your head too far backward.	Only ears should be submerged. Try to keep your hips up without tipping your head back.
	You're tipping your head too far forward.	Raise your chin so that your ears are submerged.

Problem	Reason	Solution
You're slowing down moving.	Your kick is getting slower and your legs are starting to drop, creating drag underwater.	Maintain the power and speed to your kick.
You feel your hips rocking.	This is normal and a good sign! You're most likely feeling quite sensitive to it as it's a new sensation.	**NOODLE** If you feel really unstable then hold a noodle on either side of your body rather than a kickboard against your chest.
You're unsure if you're moving.	This is normal when you're facing up.	Look for features above you to use as an indicator of if you're moving e.g. lights, windows.
You're not swimming straight.	You're tilting your head to one side.	Ensure your head is centred. Your head steers the direction you'll move towards.
	You have a dominant kick with one leg. Be aware of which way you're moving. If you're swimming towards the left then your right leg may be dominant (and vice versa).	**FINS** An option might be to wear a short blade fin on your *dominant* foot, to force your weaker foot to kick harder. This can be effective at building stamina in your weaker leg.
Your neck is hurting.	You're straining your neck as you lack trust in the water to support your head.	Relax your neck and let the water support your head. Revisit Ex 10B on back floats to understand the correct head position in the water.

Easier alternatives:

- Practise this exercise wearing a nose clip to give you more confidence if you're anxious about water entering the nose.

- **NOODLE** Practise this exercise with a noodle under your arms, rather than a kickboard against your chest (as illustrated below).

VIDEO   EXERCISE

Ex 12B: Flutter kick on back with arms by sides

Learning point:

- Moving independently on your back without any flotation aids.

NOTES

- *This may be as far as you wish to take your skills in swimming on your back.*
- *If you've a physical limitation that prevents you from adding a circular arm stroke (e.g. shoulder injury), see the easier alternative below for a way to still exercise your arms.*

Steps:

1. Repeat Ex 12A without the kickboard and with arms by your sides.

TIPS

- *Think of it as a moving back float with arms and legs together in a streamlined position.*

PROBLEM	REASON	SOLUTION
You're afraid to try without a kickboard.	You're not yet confident enough to swim independently.	NOODLE Hold a noodle on either side of your body. As you kick, try to let go of the noodles so you can transition away from them.

Easier alternative:

- If you're struggling to stay afloat with just kicking, add sculling with your upper body by simply tapping your hips with your hands.

Flutter kick on back with sculling

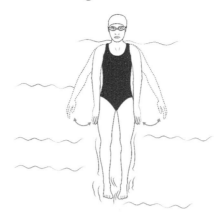

VIDEO

EXERCISE

Ex 12C: Flutter kick on back with shoulder roll

Learning points:

- How to control your balance whilst rotating your upper body.
- Multi-tasking moving upper and lower body together.

Right shoulder rolls up,
left shoulder rolls down

Left shoulder rolls up,
right shoulder rolls down

Steps:

1. Repeat Ex 12B, rolling one shoulder up towards the ceiling and dropping the other shoulder down towards the pool floor.

2. After a set of kicks, swap shoulders and repeat with your next set of kicks.

!
ALERT

Upper body rotation is crucial to avoid undue strain and possible injury to your shoulders. Rolling your shoulders will help to power your stroke.

PROBLEM	REASON	SOLUTION
You're catching water in mouth/nose.	You're rolling your head as well as your shoulders.	Keep your head still and centred; only roll your shoulders.
You find it easier to roll with one shoulder than the other.	You may have a stiff neck and/or shoulder which is causing an imbalance between your sides.	HOME Practise rolling your shoulders in circular movements to increase flexibility.

Ex 12D: Flutter kick on back with arm stroke (basic)

VIDEO   EXERCISE

Learning points:

- How to balance whilst moving your whole arm.
- Entering your arms in the water at eleven o'clock and one o'clock.

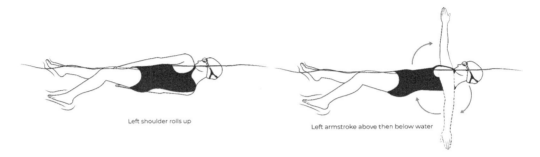

Left shoulder rolls up

Left armstroke above then below water

Steps:

1. Repeat Ex 12C but as your shoulder rolls up, follow through with your arm in the same direction. Your arm should move backwards towards your head, above the water.

2. Try to brush your ear with your arm (or get as close as possible, considering any physical limitations).

3. Move your arm underwater close to your body and return it to your side.

4. Now repeat with the other arm.

TIPS

- *A rhyme that might help is: 'Shoulder rotation then arm elevation'.*

PROBLEM	REASON	SOLUTION
You're getting water on your face.	You may be scooping water over your face with your hand.	Don't worry too much about this for now. Stroke technique is addressed in the next exercise. In the meantime exhale through mouth and nose as you lift your arm up, so water can't enter.
	You may be pulling your head backward or forward when doing the stroke, or you may be rolling your head from side to side.	Ensure only your ears are submerged and that your head remains still and centred.
You're zigzagging.	Your arm is pulling underwater too wide and shallow.	Swim alongside a wall or lane rope in order to correct a wide stroke entry, forcing a deeper underwater stroke. Make sure your arm enters behind you and digs deep, moving your arm close to your body. Imagine painting a black line on the pool floor. Focus on rolling your shoulder to bring arm closer to ear.
	You're over-extending your arm entry into the water (i.e. too flexible with shoulder roll), as illustrated on the following page*.	Your hand should enter at your shoulder line, not behind your head. Think of entering the arm wide and chances are you'll be just right!
	Your head is tilting from side to side. Your head steers the direction you'll move towards.	Ensure your head remains still and centred, and doesn't move when you stroke.
You stop moving whenever you do a stroke.	You're struggling to multi-task kicking and stroking together.	Practise!
You're wobbling and losing your balance.	You're moving your arms too fast.	Don't rush the strokes. Remember you can swim with kicking alone. Wait until one arm has returned to your thigh before starting the other. If you still struggle, space your strokes with a set of flutter kicks in between.

*Over-extending arm entry causes zigzagging

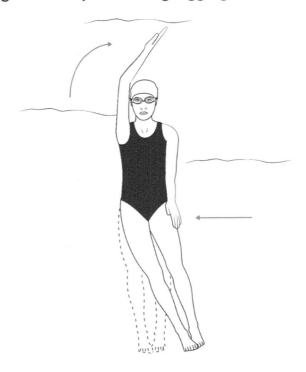

Easier alternative:

-  Hold a kickboard with one arm across your chest (as illustrated below) and practise with the other arm stroking for a set of kicks. Then switch sides.

Holding kickboard with one arm across chest (view from above)

VIDEO   EXERCISE

Ex 12E: Flutter kick on back with arm stroke (with technique)

Learning points:

- Refining your hand exit to minimise water being scooped over your face.

- Refining your hand entry to reduce splashing by 'slicing' into the water.

- Building awareness of how an effective underwater stroke can propel you.

NOTES

There are two variations of arm stroke on the back: 'straight arm pull' and 'bent arm pull'. The former is explained here as it's used for recreational swimming and is the easier one to learn.

Steps:

1. Repeat Ex 12D, focusing on exiting the water with thumb leading and palm facing inwards.

2. Enter the water with little finger first and palm facing outwards.

3. Scoop the water with palm facing upward and fingers close together. You should feel propulsion backwards as well as a lift of your hips as you scoop.

4. Repeat steps 1 to 3 with the other arm.

Easier alternative:

- KICKBOARD Hold a kickboard with one arm across your chest (as illustrated on the following page) and practise with the other arm stroking for a set of kicks. Then switch sides.

PROBLEM	REASON	SOLUTION
You're losing your balance.	You're moving your arms too fast.	Don't rush the strokes. Remember you can swim with kicking alone. Wait until one arm has returned to your thigh before starting the other. If you still struggle, space your strokes with a set of flutter kicks in between.
You're not feeling propulsion when stroking.	You're either not rolling your shoulders enough, stroking too wide, bending your elbow(s) underwater or not scooping properly.	PULLBUOY Practise with a pullbuoy to focus on the arm stroke without the kick.
Your legs are dropping.	You're forgetting to kick now that you're focusing on arm stroke technique.	Practise to multi-task kicking together with arm strokes. Raise your arms above your head and kick only on your back, to raise your hips (as illustrated below*).

PROBLEM	REASON	SOLUTION
You're getting water over face.	You're scooping water over your face (not exiting the water with thumb leading), and/or splashing your hands on top of the water (not entering the water with little finger first).	Practise!
	You're rolling your head from side to side.	Keep your head still and centred.
	You're pulling your head back when pulling up your hips.	Raise your hips but not your chin. Remember ears should be submerged.
You're worried about banging into something from behind.	This is a common concern.	An indoor pool may have ceiling flags to mark five metres before the end of the lap. If outdoor, take note of landmarks to indicate your location in the water.

*Flutter kick on back with arms above head to raise hips

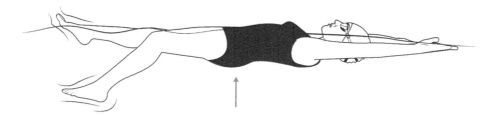

  Ex 12F: Complete 'competitive' backstroke

VIDEO   EXERCISE

Learning points:

- Learning continuous stroke action: as one arm is pulling underwater, the other is moving over water.

- Getting used to an even rocking of the shoulders as well as the rocking of the hips.

- Establishing a breathing pattern that works for you.

Steps:

1. Repeat Ex 12E without any pause between arm strokes. As one arm lifts out of the water, the other starts pulling underwater.

TIPS

- *Establish a consistent breathing pattern that works for you. Either inhaling with one stroke and exhaling with the other, or inhaling and exhaling with every stroke. Take caution not to breathe too fast as this can lead to hyperventilation and cause dizziness. Slower is better than faster.*
- *Arms should always be moving in the same direction but opposite to each other i.e. one is underwater whilst the other is above water.*

PROBLEM	REASON	SOLUTION	
You're doing strokes in pairs rather than evenly.	You've yet to establish a rhythm.	PULLBUOY	Practise with a pullbuoy to focus on a steady stroke pattern without the kick.

VIDEO

12.3 OVERVIEW OF 'SURVIVAL' BACKSTROKE

BREATHING:	as you wish (though exhalation usually takes place when kicking and pulling).
ARMS:	paired stroke (equal propulsion with legs).
LEGS:	paired whip kick (equal propulsion with arms).
PREREQUISITE:	be able to back float and stand up independently. Whip kick (see Ex 13A for technique).

VIDEO   EXERCISE

Ex 12G: Whip kick on back then glide

Learning points:

- Understanding which direction to face before starting to move on your back. (Your back should face the direction of travel.)

- How to whip kick on your back then glide streamlined.

- Understanding how your head directly affects your hips and leg positioning. (Lifting your head causes hips and legs to drop.)

- Getting used to no vision in the direction of travel. (Use landmarks instead as an indicator of your movement.)

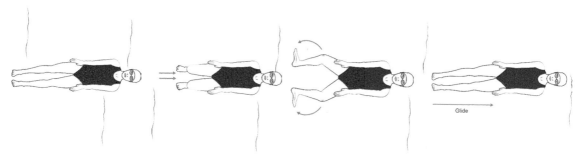

Glide

Steps:

1. Stand with your *back* facing the direction of travel.

2. Whip kick on back with arms by sides, finishing with toes pointed.

Knees should stay under the water's surface.

NOTES

Easier alternative:

- Practise this exercise with a noodle under your arms or a kickboard against your chest (as illustrated below).

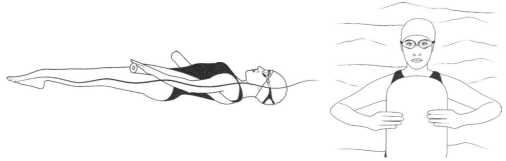

VIDEO EXERCISE

Ex 12H: Complete 'survival' backstroke

Learning point:

- Coordinating arms and legs together, by sweeping the forearms towards your thighs and whip kicking simultaneously.

NOTES

The good news here is that the arms and legs move together, which can be much easier to coordinate!

Glide

Steps:

1. Bend your elbows to sweep your hands down to your thighs as you whip kick.

2. Then glide in a streamlined position.

NOTES

Keep your elbows close to your side; only your forearms should move to minimise heat escaping your body.

13: BREASTSTROKE

13.1 OVERVIEW OF BREASTSTROKE IN GENERAL

Breaststroke is believed to be the oldest and slowest of all the strokes. In many countries around the world, it's the first stroke taught to beginners.

There are two variations of breaststroke; swimming with head submerging (referred to as 'competitive') or head permanently above the water (referred to as 'survival').

'Competitive' breaststroke isn't just swum at races! 'Competitive' breaststroke can be swum slowly and involves a relaxed *horizontal* glide. 'Survival' breaststroke involves a *more vertical* glide, creating what's called 'frontal resistance' as your body pushes against the water with head up. This can make it more tiring to swim.

TIPS

Many of my students who wish to swim 'survival' breaststroke, first learn 'competitive' breaststroke, which makes it easier to then transition to swimming with your head up. You may skip to learn 'survival' only in Ex 13H, but you'll still need to master the whip kick (Ex 13C) and arm stroke (Ex 13E) first.

13.2 ADVANTAGES OF 'COMPETITIVE' BREASTSTROKE

- Energy conserving because it's a slow stroke that involves gliding through water.

- More relaxing for your neck and back (compared with 'survival' breaststroke).

13.3 ADVANTAGES OF 'SURVIVAL' BREASTSTROKE

- Ability to breathe as you wish, so may be preferred if you aren't comfortable getting your face wet.

- You can keep your hair dry or wear sunglasses as your head is above water permanently.

- Full peripheral vision of your surroundings e.g. when at the beach.

VIDEO

13.4 OVERVIEW OF 'COMPETITIVE' BREASTSTROKE

BREATHING:	to the front (one stroke per breath).
ARMS:	paired stroke (less propulsion).
LEGS:	paired whip kick (majority of propulsion).
PREREQUISITE:	able to front float and stand up independently.

VIDEO   EXERCISE

Ex 13A: Whip kick by pool edge/ladder

Learning points:

- How to whip kick; a paired and flowing leg action which can be the most difficult component of the stroke to learn.

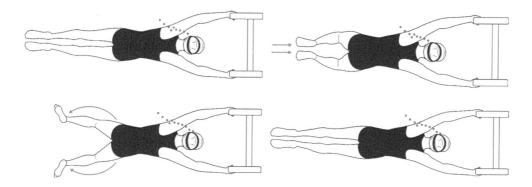

Steps:

1. Hold the pool edge/ladder and exhale face down, letting your legs float up to their highest point under the water's surface.

2. Bring your legs together and straight.

3. Bend your knees to bring your heels (not toes) to your bottom, turn your toes out towards the side with soles facing upwards in V position. Heels push back and outwards, kick out to hip width apart with ankles flexed, then whip legs back together.

4. Finish with legs together and straight.

TIPS

- *It can be difficult to know if you've done this kick correctly. You should feel your body move towards the pool edge/ladder if your kick is correct.*
- *Kick backwards not downwards. Think heels towards your bottom, not knees towards chest.*

NOTES

At step 3, your ankles should be flexed, with toes pointing outwards and curled towards your knees. If you have difficulty flexing only at step 3, practise the whole exercise with feet flexed; and then transition to flexing only during the kick out phase.

PROBLEM	REASON	SOLUTION
One or both feet are splashing on top of the water's surface.	Your legs have floated too high.	Look slightly forward, to drop your legs so your heels are just under the water's surface.
	One or both feet are floppy.	Focus on flexing the ankle to keep the foot *under* the water. Turn toes to face out towards the sides.
Your legs are dropping.	You're bending your knees towards your chest rather than bringing heels towards your bottom.	SNORKEL — Practise the kick with a snorkel. HOME — Practise the kick lying face down on your bed or sofa. It'll then be impossible to bend your knees towards your chest!
	You're looking forward rather than downward, causing your hips and legs to drop.	Tuck chin in. Imagine your head is an iceberg, with only one third of it (the back of your head) above the water's surface.
You can't flex your ankles.	Either due to restrictions in your mobility, or due to unfamiliarity of this positioning.	Ironically as you stand from being on your front, your feet naturally flex slightly in order to put your feet flat on the pool floor (as illustrated below*). Stand on one leg with your back against the wall and place the other foot as high as possible flat against the wall. This is the flex required.
Your kick is circling in the reverse direction.	You're getting confused with the movement of the whip.	Think 'kick out, snap in'.
VIDEO — You're only turning out one foot when you kick, i.e. one foot kicks correctly and the other provides no propulsion.	You have a 'screw kick'. This could be due to restricted mobility with either one hip or one knee.	HOME — Practise the kick lying face down in front of a mirror. Focus on legs and feet moving symmetrically.

PROBLEM	REASON	SOLUTION
Your legs are not straight at the end of the kick.	You're rushing the kick.	Remember to start and finish with your legs together and straight. Focus on either ankles or heels touching each other after every kick (to ensure your legs snap together).

*Flexing your feet as you stand

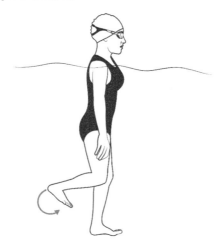

Easier alternative:

- KICKBOARD NOODLE Practise on your back (if you're confident enough) with a noodle under your arms or kickboard against your chest (as illustrated). This way you can concentrate only on the kick without having to worry about breath control. Look up and not at your feet!

Whip kick on back with noodle

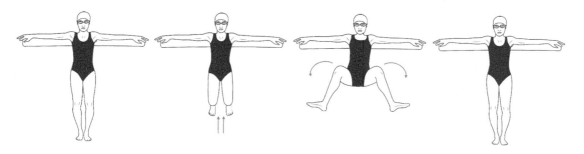

VIDEO

EXERCISE

Ex 13B: Whip kick with kickboard

Training aid:
KICKBOARD

Learning point:

- Building good technique of looking downward rather than forward, so your face doesn't create 'frontal resistance' and slow down the propulsion generated by the kick.

Steps:

1. Repeat Ex 13A holding a kickboard instead of the pool edge/ladder.

2. Stand up to inhale *before* you run out of air.

PROBLEM	REASON	SOLUTION
You're not moving.	You lack speed or power to your kick. You may be thinking of the kick in two parts (the push back and the snap in). Think of it as one complete and smooth kick!	SNORKEL — Practise with a snorkel. Push the water backwards with force using the soles of your feet.
		KICKBOARD NOODLE Practise on your back (if you're confident enough) with a noodle under your arms or kickboard against your chest. This way you can concentrate only on the kick without having to worry about breath control. Look up and not at your feet! See the last two illustrations of Ex 13A.
You're moving at a tangent.	You have a weak leg or loose ankle.	Kick with balanced power, flexing both feet.
	One leg is kicking ahead of the other.	SNORKEL — Practise with a snorkel and focus on a paired kick.

PROBLEM	REASON	SOLUTION
You're feeling wobbly.	Your hips aren't parallel to the pool floor before the kick.	Ensure you're balanced on your front before kicking.

Harder alternative:

- Practise this exercise without a kickboard and with arms outstretched instead.

  Ex 13C: Whip kick with kickboard then glide

VIDEO   EXERCISE

Training aid:

KICKBOARD

Learning points

- Improving efficiency by gliding after every kick: 'Kick to glide'.

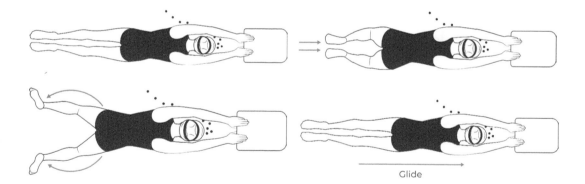

Glide

Steps:

1. Repeat Ex 13B, incorporating a streamlined glide after every kick.

PROBLEM	REASON	SOLUTION
You're not gliding.	You may not be finishing with legs together and straight.	To glide you must be streamlined. Focus on either ankles or heels touching each other after every kick.

PROBLEM	REASON	SOLUTION
You're not gliding. (cont.)	You may lack the speed or power to your kick. You may be thinking of the kick in two parts; the push back and the snap in. Think of it as one complete and smooth kick.	KICKBOARD NOODLE Practise on your back (if you're confident enough) with a noodle under your arms or kickboard against your chest. This way you can concentrate only on the kick without having to worry about breath control. Look up and not at your feet! See the last two illustrations of Ex 13A.
Your legs are dropping.	You're waiting too long to kick again after the glide.	Kick as soon as you start to lose momentum from the glide.
You're flutter kicking (up and down) in between the whip kick.	You're not kicking with enough power to glide and therefore feel the need to move the legs to avoid sinking.	Focus on increasing the power and speed of the whip kick so you can maintain horizontal positioning.

  Ex 13D: Breaststroke arms with noodle (basic)

VIDEO   EXERCISE

Training aid:

NOODLE

Learning points:

- Understanding how to use your arms to inhale.

- Understanding how far to raise your head to inhale. (If your head is too high when inhaling, your legs will drop and you'll start to sink. If your head is too low when inhaling, you'll catch water in mouth and/or nose.)

- *Think: one pull one breath or 'pull to breathe'.*
- *If you find your lower body sinking, use two noodles rather than one.*

TIPS

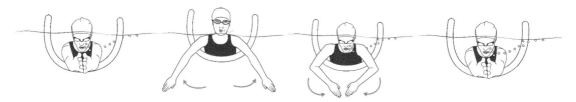

Steps:

1. Place the noodle across your chest and under your arms.

2. Inhale then exhale slowly face down, with arms together outstretched in front of you, and legs apart. Floating with your lower body will help you to maintain your balance (as illustrated below).

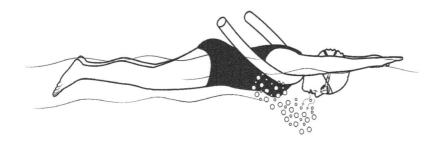

3. When ready to inhale, sweep your arms around in a circular motion, pulling outwards and downwards shoulder width apart with palms facing outward. Look forward to raise your mouth and nose above the water.

4. After inhalation, exhale face down with your arms outstretched again like an arrow.

TIPS

Think of 'Blowing your hands forward'.

NOTES

Raise your head only to chin level (to be able to inhale through mouth above water).

PROBLEM	REASON	SOLUTION
Your back hurts.	You're using your back to raise your head above water.	Focus on using your arms to inhale.

PROBLEM	REASON	SOLUTION
You're catching water.	You're waiting too long to come up for air.	Stroke to inhale *before* you run out of air.
	You're opening your mouth too early.	Only open your mouth when it's above the water level.
	Your arms aren't pushing downwards enough.	Focus on a sweeping circular downward motion with the arms to clear the mouth of the water level.
You're not getting enough or any air.	You're breathing in too late or not at all due to fear of catching water. This is very common.	Lift head as arms pull apart. Think of the stroke and breath as a single movement. **SNORKEL** Practise 'pull to breathe' with a snorkel to build your confidence in ensuring you're clearing the water level every time (whilst inhaling through the tube).
	You're not exhaling enough to have the capacity to inhale.	Concentrate on blowing bubbles when face down.
You're sinking.	You fear catching water and are pushing down with your arms excessively. This raises your head too high and causes your lower body to drop.	Adjust the angle of your stroke to be wider and shallower so that you only just clear your mouth of the water level to inhale. I.e. Stay more horizontal when inhaling.
	You're looking forward when you exhale, causing your lower body to drop.	Always face down when exhaling, chin tucked in.

Easier alternative:

- Practise this exercise walking, without the noodle.

Harder alternatives:

- Practise this exercise with noodle across hips instead of under your arms.

- Practise this exercise with a pullbuoy instead of a noodle.

VIDEO EXERCISE

Ex 13E: Breaststroke arms with noodle (with technique)

Training aid:

NOODLE

Learning point:

- Refining breaststroke arm technique.

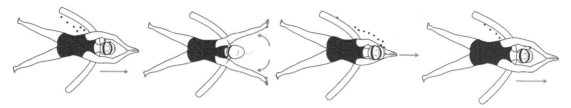

Steps:

1. Repeat Ex 13D: drawing two narrow semi-circles *under* the water's surface (there should be no splashing) using your elbows as levers. Your arms should not touch your thighs i.e. your hands shouldn't sweep out more than shoulder width apart.

2. As your hands meet close to your body, extend to a fully stretched position by moving them away from your body with either index fingers touching (like an open book) or palms together (like in prayer), as illustrated below. This ensures your hands don't criss-cross each other.

Two options of hand positions

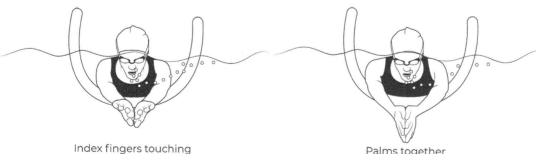

Index fingers touching   Palms together

TIPS

- *Think of drawing an upside down heart with your hands.*

• *The noodle helps to restrict your arms from sweeping out too wide.*

VIDEO   EXERCISE

Ex 13F: Whip kicking and stroking with noodle ('kick, glide, pull & breathe')

Training aid:

NOODLE

Learning points:

• Coordinating legs, arms and breathing together in the order of: 'Kick, glide, pull, breathe'.

When either the arm pull or leg kick takes place, the opposite end of the body remains still and streamlined.

TIPS

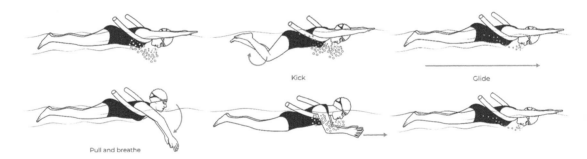

Kick

Glide

Pull and breathe

Steps:

1. Place noodle across your chest and under your arms.

2. Inhale and exhale face down with arms and legs together and straight.

3. Whip kick then glide, propelling your streamlined body forward.

4. Then with legs together, pull and breathe.

• *Think 'Kick out, breathe out'.*

TIPS

PROBLEM	REASON	SOLUTION
You're pulling and kicking simultaneously.	This is a common fault. It may feel instinctive but it's not correct.	Front float first to 'reset'. Bring arms and legs together streamlined. Focus on lower body ('kick and glide') then upper body ('pull and breathe').
		Interlock thumbs when doing the kick in order to stop arms moving.
		Instead of 'kick glide, pull, breathe', practise 'kick, glide, kick, glide, pull, breathe'. This will get you used to not moving your arms whilst kicking.
		Practise with a snorkel to help with coordination of strokes and kicking. SNORKEL
		Practise the order of 'kick, glide, pull, breathe' lying face down. HOME
You're propelling yourself with arms and not legs.	You've lost the power or technique to your kick and are over-depending on your arms. It's common to lose the flex to your kick when arms are added.	Revisit Ex 13C.
The noodle keeps slipping up towards your chest.	You're pushing down and pivoting your body up too high to inhale.	Adjust the angle of your stroke to be wider and shallower so that you only just clear your mouth of the water level to inhale.
		I.e. Stay more horizontal when inhaling.

Harder alternative:

- Practise this exercise with noodle across hips instead of under your arms.

Ex 13G: Complete 'competitive' breaststroke

VIDEO   EXERCISE

Learning points:

- Transitioning away from aids.

- Understanding how kick timing is crucial. Kick too soon and you'll kick downward. Kick too late and your legs will have sunk.

TIPS

The fewer the kicks, the more efficient you are: so try to count how many kicks you do over a certain distance and then aim to reduce that number. Think about maximising every length of glide.

Steps:

1. Repeat Ex 13F without the noodle.

PROBLEM	REASON	SOLUTION
You're not swimming straight.	One arm or one leg is stronger than the other.	If you're swimming towards the left, then your right stroke or right kick is stronger. Or vice versa.
You're propelling yourself with arms and not legs.	You've lost the power or technique to your kick and are over-depending on your arms.	NOODLE SNORKEL To refocus on your kick, practise on your back (with or without a noodle) or with a snorkel on your front, trying to touch your heels with your hands (as illustrated on the following page)*. Instead of 'kick glide, pull, breathe', practise 'kick, glide, kick, glide', to refocus on the kick.

PROBLEM	REASON	SOLUTION
You're sinking too low to be able to resurface for air.	Your kick isn't powerful enough.	Focus on *whip* kick: stronger and quicker.
	You're waiting too long to kick.	As soon as you've stroked to inhale, exhale face down and kick with arms outstretched.
	Your head is looking forward when you exhale, causing hips and legs to drop.	Ensure you exhale with chin down to raise legs.
	Your stroke may be too vertical or your head is coming up too high, pivoting your body up too high and causing your lower body to drop.	Adjust the angle of your stroke to be wider and shallower so that you only just clear your mouth of the water level to inhale. I.e. Stay more horizontal when inhaling.
You're feeling wobbly.	Your glide is too long or your kick isn't strong enough.	Pull and breathe *before* your glide loses momentum, or kick stronger.
You feel like you're too submerged.	This is common as it's difficult to know where your head's at when exhaling face down! It can often be a misconception.	So long as you can come up for air, you're not too low.

*Whip kick touching heels with hands whilst wearing a snorkel

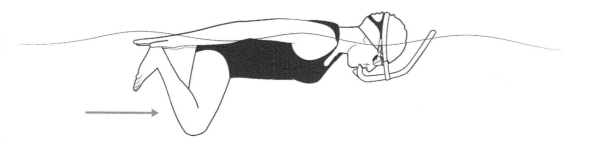

13.5 OVERVIEW OF 'SURVIVAL' BREASTSTROKE

BREATHING:	as you wish (establish a comfortable rhythm with yourstrokes).
ARMS:	paired stroke (less propulsion).
LEGS:	paired whip kick (majority of propulsion).
PREREQUISITE:	whip kick (Ex 13C) and breaststroke arm stroke (Ex 13E).

  ## Ex 13H: Complete 'survival' breaststroke

Training aid:

NOODLE

Steps:

1. Practise Ex 13F with head permanently up (noodle under arms).

2. Practise Ex 13F with head permanently up (noodle across hips).

3. Then transition away from the noodle to swim independently.

TIPS

Remember to keep breathing!

NOTES

- *Alternative way to swim survival breaststroke:*
  *If you find it difficult to coordinate moving arms and legs separately, you could move them simultaneously. This means kicking and pulling together without much glide. **It's technically incorrect** but may be easier to do, albeit more tiring.*

14: FREESTYLE

14.1 OVERVIEW OF FREESTYLE

BREATHING:	to the side. Either bilateral (alternating sides, three or five strokes per breath) or unilateral (same side, two or four strokes per breath)*.
ARMS:	continuous alternating stroke (majority of propulsion).
LEGS:	continuous alternating flutter kick (less propulsion).
PREREQUISITE:	be able to front float and stand up independently.

*The correct way is bilateral breathing, three strokes per breath.

Freestyle, otherwise known as 'front crawl', is the fastest and most efficient stroke. It's considered the most challenging to learn in terms of multi-tasking kicking, stroking and breathing altogether.

It's the stroke which is commonly perceived as the definition of swimming here in Australia. It's not unusual for students to tell me they can swim breaststroke or backstroke but cannot swim 'properly' as they don't know how to freestyle!

14.2 ADVANTAGES OF BILATERAL BREATHING

- **Better flexibility and balance** in your body. Any pre-existing conditions such as a stiff neck or shoulder could be exacerbated by breathing on only the easier side.

- To empower you with the **skill to change which side** you inhale on.

  e.g. You can switch to breathing on a different side based on wave conditions or the sun's position in the open water.

14.3 ADVANTAGES OF UNILATERAL BREATHING

- To master swimming freestyle quicker when you find it easier to turn to one particular side to inhale. Perhaps you simply wish to swim freestyle for survival reasons.

- To accommodate a respiratory condition like asthma where you're more prone to breathlessness and need to breathe more frequently (on the second rather than third stroke).

NOTES

You may wish to learn how to inhale on both sides but find that it's too difficult to inhale on the third stroke. If this is the case, you can still maintain balance and flexibility on both sides of your body by inhaling only towards the left for one set (a certain distance based on your ability), and only towards the right for the next set.

VIDEO   EXERCISE

Ex 14A: Flutter kick on front with kickboard

Training aid: or
KICKBOARD   NOODLE

Learning points:

- How to flutter kick on your front in a horizontal, streamlined position and get used to a rocking of the hips.

- How to kick and exhale at the same time.

- Understanding how your head directly affects your hips and leg positioning. (Lifting your head slightly causes hips and legs to drop.) Therefore the importance of ensuring your eyes look down to the bottom of the pool, not forwards.

TIPS

- *The T-shaped black line will indicate if you're getting close to the wall. Remember the kickboard will bump into the wall before you do!*
- *Think of the flutter kick like a butterfly flutters its wings; small and fast.*

NOTES

You may find that you have a different style (movement/speed) of flutter kick on your front compared with your back. This is common and will simply require practise to bring consistency on both sides.

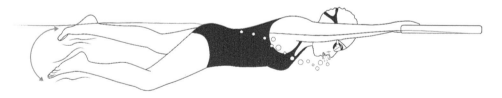

Steps:

1. Hold the kickboard with hands at the bottom or the sides (as illustrated). The latter allows more room for your head to turn.

2. Review the steps to get on your front with a front float (Chapter 10 'Floating horizontally').

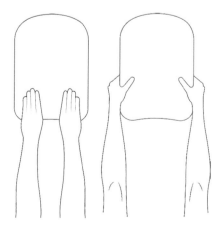

3. Bring legs together in a streamlined position and start kicking up and down in an alternating continuous action from your hips (not knees), ideally breaking your heels at the water's surface. Your knees should bend slightly with loose ankles and floppy feet.

4. As you get low on air, lean backwards and bend your knees to stand up.

PROBLEM	REASON	SOLUTION
You're not moving.	You're bending your knees excessively (using calf muscles rather than thigh muscles). This is called a bicycle kick, as illustrated below.	Kick from the hips and point your toes to straighten your legs. Think of flicking your feet rather than pedalling. FINS A pair of short blade fins can help to straighten your kick, however you'll need to practise getting used to wearing them first and standing with them from a front float.
	You're not bending your knees enough. Your legs are too stiff.	Try to relax and bend your knees a little.
	Your legs are too low. Either you started too early (before your legs had reached their highest float) or you waited too long to start kicking (your legs started to drop after floating).	Bring legs together and start kicking when they're at their highest position in the float.
	You have a weak kick or big kick.	Kick fast and small.
	Your hips have dropped.	Push your bottom up towards the water's surface; so your body straightens out and becomes more horizontal. Tuck your chin in to help raise your legs.
	Your legs are far apart.	Kick with your legs together; a streamlined position is important to minimise resistance in the water.

PROBLEM	REASON	SOLUTION
You're not moving. (cont.)	Your legs are kicking sideways.	Kick up and down.
	You're looking forward rather than downward, causing your hips and legs to drop.	Tuck chin in. Imagine your head is an iceberg, with only one third of it (the back of your head) above the water's surface.
	Your ankles are stiff/flexed with toes curled up. This is common if you're an experienced runner or cyclist.	Kick with loose ankles and floppy feet, pointing your toes. A pair of short blade fins FINS can help to loosen your ankles, however you'll need to practise getting used to wearing them first and standing with them from a front float.
You're getting water in your mouth and/or nose.	You're not exhaling long enough from your mouth and/or nose.	Exhale all the time unless you're inhaling.
	You're not exhaling strong enough from your mouth and/or nose. Weak bubbles can let the water enter.	Push air out harder through your mouth and/or nose.
You're slowing down moving.	Your kick is getting slower and your legs are starting to drop, creating drag underwater.	Maintain the power and speed to your kick.
You feel your hips rocking.	This is normal and a good sign! You're most likely feeling quite sensitive to it as it's a new sensation.	NOODLE If you feel really unstable then hold a noodle on either side of your body, rather than a kickboard in front of you.
You're moving at a tangent.	You're tilting your head to one side.	Ensure your head is centred. Your head steers the direction you'll move towards.
	You're not holding the kickboard straight in front of you. You have a dominant kick with one leg. Be aware of which way you're skewing. If you're swimming towards the left then your right leg may be dominant (and vice versa).	Ensure the kickboard stays centred. It steers the direction you'll move towards. An option might be to wear FINS a short blade fin on your dominant foot, to force your weaker foot to kick harder. This can be effective at building muscle memory and stamina in your weaker leg.

Bicycle kick with kickboard (incorrect due to excessive knee bend)

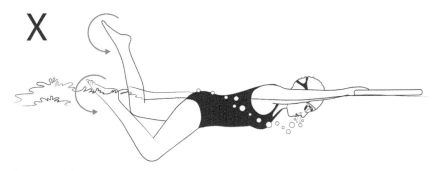

Easier alternative:

- Practise this exercise kicking, holding onto pool edge/ladder.

Ex 14B: Flutter kick on front with kickboard and breathing (up)

Training aid: KICKBOARD

Learning points:

- How to multi-task kicking and breathing (exhaling and inhaling).

- Understanding your lung capacity to inhale *before* your lungs are empty.
  If you inhale too late, you'll be desperate and gasping.
  If you inhale too early, you won't have expelled enough air to have the capacity to breathe in properly.

- Understanding how your head directly affects your hips and leg positioning. (Lifting your head slightly causes hips and legs to drop).

Steps:

1. Repeat Ex 14A but instead of standing as you get low on air, look forward to clear your mouth and nose above the water level and inhale. Don't stop kicking!

2. Exhale face down, kicking continuously throughout.

NOTES

- *Your first exhalation will take longer than any other. This is because your first inhalation was taken when standing and was therefore the biggest.*
- *As your head lifts to inhale, your legs will start to drop as your body works on a pivot. Maintain a strong kick to stay horizontal!*

TIPS

- *Don't worry about the number of kicks per breath; this over complicates things. Just ensure you only breathe in once per lift of the head.*

PROBLEM	REASON	SOLUTION
You find yourself standing after looking forward to inhale.	Your head is coming up too high when you inhale, causing your legs to drop.	Don't push down on the kickboard and raise your head/shoulders any higher than clearing your mouth of the water level.
	You're stopping the kick when inhaling.	Practise multi-tasking your kicking and breathing together.
Your head is up for a long time.	You're breathing in and out a few times above water, rather than *one single* inhalation.	Inhale only ONCE: think *one* breath in, *one* breath out.
You're catching water.	You're opening your mouth too soon to inhale before it has cleared the water level.	Inhale deeper/exhale slower/raise your head sooner to inhale.
You're rushing the breathing.	Kicking can cause people to increase the speed of breathing.	Practise to maintain a more controlled breathing speed.

Easier alternatives:

- Practise this exercise standing; holding onto pool edge/ladder/step.

- Practise this exercise walking; holding a kickboard with arms outstretched.

- Practise this exercise kicking; holding onto pool edge/ladder.

VIDEO   EXERCISE

Ex 14C: Flutter kick on front with kickboard and breathing (to the side)

Training aid:

KICKBOARD

Learning points:

- How to maintain a horizontal body position when inhaling, as the head now *turns* rather than *lifts*.

- Understanding how far to roll your head to the side in order to clear your mouth and nose of the water.

- Maintaining a still and centred head position, only turning to inhale.

TIPS

- *Think of four H's: hands, head, hips and heels all in a horizontal position.*

NOTES

- *If you have poor shoulder or neck flexibility and find this exercise too challenging, skip to Ex 14D.*

Steps:

1. Repeat Ex 14B, but instead of inhaling looking up, inhale to the side with chin tucked in.

TIPS

- *Keep your head low when side breathing; with ear to shoulder or part of your lower goggle submerged.*
- *Practise turning to the same side repetitively to build your confidence i.e. a set turning towards the right to inhale, then a set turning towards the left to inhale. If you're Swimmer A (beginner with fear), turn your head to face the pool edge when inhaling in order to know that you're within arm's reach to grab the side if you panic or struggle.*

NOTES

- *You may find it's easier to turn on one side than the other. Having an easier side doesn't mean it's necessarily better: it can mean your head is lifting (which is why you find it easier to inhale) or it could lead to you catching water as you're less focused. Ironically people can have better technique on the side that they find more difficult, as they're concentrating more!*

PROBLEM	REASON	SOLUTION
You're unsure how far to roll your head.	This is a new movement and you may be anxious about catching water.	Start with your head *on the side*. Inhale then roll your head to exhale face down. Now try to return your head position back to where you started *on the side*.
Your legs spread wide apart when side breathing.	It's easier to balance with legs apart (just like when floating) but it's more difficult to move forward efficiently when you're not streamlined.	Practise a stronger kick with legs together to maintain balance when you turn to the side.
Your head lifts to breathe in.	You're worried about catching water.	Try to look over your shoulder to ensure your head stays low when turning.
	You're pushing down on the kickboard to inhale.	Make sure you're holding the kickboard at the sides or bottom; and not with your hand placed on top of the kickboard. Refer to Chapter 6.8 'Equipment to use' for illustrations.
	Don't look forward when exhaling; otherwise your head will automatically lift as you turn.	Tuck your chin in when exhaling. It will take longer to roll to clear the water, but this is normal and correct.
Your head sometimes lifts and sometimes stays low when turning.	You're struggling to get the consistency with the head position when inhaling.	Choose a focal point on the side to revert your eyes to every time you inhale.
You can't kick and side breathe together.	You're struggling with the multi-tasking.	Revert back to Ex 14B to practise multi-tasking breathing and kicking.

PROBLEM	REASON	SOLUTION
You're feeling wobbly.	You have a weak kick.	Focus on a strong kick to help you to balance.
You're not getting any air.	You're turning to the side but not inhaling due to lack of confidence in getting air and not water.	Refer to easier alternatives (below).
You're looking forward to inhale rather than to the side.	You're pausing to inhale which is a sign of lack of confidence.	Force yourself to only turn *when* you need to inhale.
	You're worried about bumping into something ahead of you.	Remember that the kickboard will bump into anything before your head!
You're gasping for air.	You're turning too late.	Turn earlier, *before* your lungs are empty.
	You're exhaling too fast.	Exhale slower.
	You're rushing the inhalation.	Refer to easier alternatives (below).

Easier alternatives:

- Practise this exercise standing; holding onto pool edge/ladder/step.

- Practise this exercise walking; holding a kickboard with arms outstretched.

- Practise this exercise kicking; holding onto pool edge/ladder.

VIDEO   EXERCISE

Ex 14D: Flutter kick on front with kickboard and shoulder roll

Training aid:

KICKBOARD

Learning points:

- How to maintain balance with one hand (rather than two) controlling the kickboard.

- How to rotate your upper body as well as your head.

Steps:

1. Hold the kickboard with one hand. Hold it in the middle and at the bottom (as illustrated). Your other arm should be permanently down at your side.

It's important to hold the kickboard in the middle for stability.

1. Inhale then exhale face down and flutter kick.

2. As your head turns to the side to inhale, roll your shoulder back and open up your chest. Keep your ear touching the shoulder of your extended arm (that's holding the kickboard) so your head stays low with the turn.

TIPS

- *Practise turning to the same side repetitively to build your confidence i.e. a set turning towards the right to inhale, then a set turning towards the left to inhale.*

PROBLEM	REASON	SOLUTION
You're catching water when trying to inhale.	You're not turning far enough onto your side.	Focus on rolling your shoulder back and opening up your chest. **KICKBOARD** Practise swimming only in the second position of the illustration above (i.e. kicking on your side with mouth and nose above water level). This is a demanding drill that requires you to engage your core, kick strongly and keep your ear on your shoulder so your head doesn't lift and your legs don't drop. Don't worry about speed: focus on technique.
	You're opening your mouth too early to inhale.	Don't rush the breath in; ensure you've cleared the water before inhaling.
You're losing your balance when trying to inhale.	You're turning too far onto your side and tipping onto your back.	Focus on turning only far enough to clear your mouth and nose of the water level.

Easier alternative:

- Practise this exercise kicking, holding onto pool edge/ladder.

VIDEO EXERCISE

Ex 14E: Flutter kick on front with kickboard, one stroke per breath (basic)

Training aid: or

KICKBOARD NOODLE

Learning points:

- How to use your arm when you need to inhale.

TIPS

Don't worry about where your hand or arm is when inhaling! Simply think of a single movement: pull and inhale together.

NOTES

- *Only stroke when you need to turn to inhale.*
- *You may find it easier to breathe compared with Ex 14D, as your arm can now help to roll your body and head to the side.*

Steps:

1. Hold the board with two hands at the bottom (as illustrated).

   (This is important because if you hold the board on the sides, you'll lose your balance once you remove one hand to do a stroke as your weight will tip to one side).

2. Exhale face down and flutter kick.

3. As you get low on air, pull one arm underwater and inhale then return your hand back to the board above the water as you exhale.

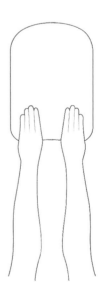

NOTES

- *Both hands should always be holding the board except during the turn to inhale when one hand comes off.*

TIPS

- *Practise turning to the same side repetitively to build your confidence i.e. a set turning towards the right to stroke and inhale, then a set turning towards the left to stroke and inhale.*

PROBLEM	REASON	SOLUTION
You're using one arm to stroke but breathing on the other side.	Lack of coordination.	Think about moving your arm out of the way to inhale.
You're feeling wobbly.	Weak kick.	Maintain a strong kick. Just remember a stronger kick shouldn't mean faster strokes!
Your stroke and breathing aren't in sync.	Lack of coordination.	For this exercise, your breathing should dictate when your arm moves.
You can't swim straight.	Your kickboard isn't straight. This can happen when your weaker (non-dominant arm) is holding the kickboard.	Practise!
Your kicks are faster when turning.	Lack of confidence that you won't clear the water to inhale.	Practise!
Your kicks are slower when turning.	You're struggling to multi-task stroking, inhaling and kicking together.	Practise!
You're pausing to inhale.	Lack of confidence that you won't clear the water to inhale.	Practise!
You're not getting enough air.	Your stroke is too fast.	Stroke slower to allow more time to inhale.
	Your breath is too shallow or late.	Focus on a deeper or earlier inhalation.

Easier alternative:

- Practise this exercise with a noodle across your hips to help keep you horizontal. Here's a reminder of the steps to use both the kickboard and noodle together.

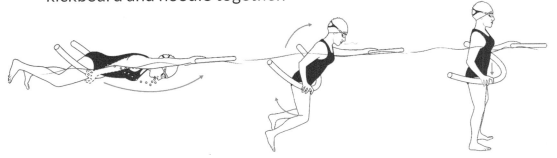

VIDEO   EXERCISE

Ex 14F: Flutter kick on front with kickboard, one stroke per breath (with technique)

Training aid:

KICKBOARD

Learning point:

- Understanding how an effective stroke propels you. Your body should jerk forward whenever you stroke, compared to when you're kicking and exhaling only.

Steps:

1. Repeat Ex 14E with the below stroke technique.

Under the water:
As you run low on air, let go of the kickboard with one hand, roll your shoulder down and scoop the water backwards, with a slight elbow-bend. The stroke should be deep and pass close to your body, with a firm wrist to propel you forwards.

Over the water:
As your hand reaches your hip, roll your shoulder up, raising your arm out of the water *with your elbow first*. Reach forward over the water's surface to hold the kickboard again.

TIPS

Lead with your elbow not your hand; your elbow should always be higher than your wrist.

ALERT

Upper body rotation is crucial to avoid undue strain and possible injury to your shoulders. Rolling your shoulder down then up means you lean forwards and backwards using your body weight to power your stroke.

Easier alternatives:

- Practise this exercise standing, holding onto pool edge/ladder/step.
- Practise this exercise kicking, holding onto pool edge/ladder.
- Practise this exercise walking, holding a kickboard.

PROBLEM	REASON	SOLUTION
You're finding you have less time to inhale.	This is a good sign that you're stroking correctly. You'll indeed have a shorter time to inhale compared with a straight arm pull in Ex 14E.	Anticipate the turn and inhalation. Practise to get used to this shorter timeframe to inhale.
You're flicking your hand back.	This can happen, there's no reason for it though!	Focus on raising your elbow rather than using your hand to flick as you exit the water.
Your hand/arm is skimming across the water before you reach forward to hold the kickboard.	Your elbow is dropping above the water.	Roll your shoulder up higher and raise your elbow so your hand and arm are fully clear above the water. Think of 'reaching over the barrel'.
Your stroke isn't propelling you forward.	You have a shallow or wide stroke. This is common on your weaker/non-dominant side.	Ensure the stroke is deep and close to your body.
	You're not using your elbow as a lever underwater.	Ensure there's a slight bend to your elbow as you pull through underwater.
	Your wrist is bent or fingers are spread out, resulting in not effectively scooping the water back with your hand.	Ensure your wrist is firm with palm facing backward and fingers are close together.

VIDEO   EXERCISE

Ex 14G: Flutter kick on front with kickboard, two strokes per breath

Training aid:

KICKBOARD

Learning points:

- How to stroke when exhaling.
- How to adapt your breathing to fit in with your stroke pattern.

Steps:

1. Repeat Ex 14F but when you exhale, stroke with your second arm e.g. right stroke to inhale, then left stroke to exhale.

TIPS

Practise turning to the same side repetitively to build your confidence i.e. a set using both arms and turning towards the right to inhale, then a set using both arms and turning towards the left to inhale.

NOTES

- *It's a common fault for your stroke to be higher when you inhale compared to when you exhale. This is because you subconsciously raise your arm higher to move it out of the way in order to inhale. However both strokes should look exactly the same; whether exhaling or inhaling.*

PROBLEM	REASON	SOLUTION
You still have air to exhale before you turn to inhale.	You're still learning to adapt your breathing to fit in with your stroke pattern.	Exhale stronger so that you need to inhale sooner.
You've got a slower or straighter stroke when you inhale.	You're pausing to inhale.	Practise. Consider moving on to Ex 14H when you'll be inhaling every three strokes (rather than every two). You'll need to move your arms faster per breath which is likely to force an elbow bend!

PROBLEM	REASON	SOLUTION
Your strokes are in pairs (like the rhythm of a heartbeat) rather than at an even pace throughout.	You're still learning to adapt your breathing to fit in with your stroke pattern.	As soon as you've stroked with one arm, catch the board and stroke with the other arm. This will even out your stroke rhythm and help to adapt your breathing accordingly.

VIDEO EXERCISE

Ex 14H: Flutter kick on front with kickboard, three strokes per breath

Training aid:

KICKBOARD

Learning points:

- How to breathe bilaterally; alternating sides of inhalation. This is the correct 'textbook' way to swim freestyle.

- How to adapt your breathing to fit in with a new stroke pattern.

TIPS

Think: '1, 2 then breathe on 3ʳᵈ', or 'exhale, exhale, inhale' or 'two strokes face down, one stroke face up' or 'inhale on 3ʳᵈ pull'.

NOTES

If you opt to only breathe on the one side, then you can skip this exercise.

Steps:

1. Repeat Ex 14G but exhale for two strokes rather than one.

TIPS

Inhale more and/or exhale slower so you have enough air to expel for two strokes rather than just one stroke.

NOTES

It doesn't matter which arm you start the exercise with, as you'll naturally alternate sides to inhale.

PROBLEM	REASON	SOLUTION
You're confused about when to inhale.	You're still learning to adapt your breathing to fit in with your stroke pattern.	For the moment, keep counting. It'll become automated with more practice.

Easier alternatives:

- Practise this exercise standing, holding onto pool edge/ladder.

- Practise this exercise kicking, holding onto pool edge/ladder.

- Practise this exercise walking, holding a kickboard with arms outstretched.

- Practise this exercise with a noodle across your hips. The noodle isn't an obstruction to your strokes – it's correcting your stroke by prompting you to bend your elbow to lift your arm out of the water.

  ## Ex 14I: Freestyle using one side of body

VIDEO   EXERCISE

Training aid:

KICKBOARD

Learning points:

- Transitioning slightly away from the kickboard.

- Getting familiar with the pace and smoothness of complete freestyle by swimming it with one side of your body.

- Learning when and how your hand should enter the water.

Steps:

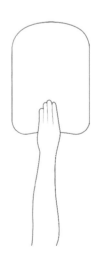

1. Hold the kickboard with one hand in the middle and at the bottom (as illustrated).

   (It's important to hold the kickboard in the middle for stability).

2. Exhale face down and flutter kick. Stroke continuously with the same arm *without touching the kickboard.* Your hand should enter the water in

front of your head (in line with your shoulder) and with *fingertips first* by keeping your elbow high.

3. Inhale on the second, third or fourth stroke (depending on which stroke pattern you've chosen).

NOTES

You may find you have a dominant and weak side. If you're right-handed, you may find it more difficult to breathe towards the right as you're holding the kickboard with your weaker (left) hand.

PROBLEM	REASON	SOLUTION
Your stroke when inhaling is slower than the strokes when exhaling.	You're pausing to inhale.	Inhale quicker or slow down the strokes when exhaling to ensure an even stroke pace overall.
You're splashing the water when stroking.	You're dropping your elbow above the water or slapping the water with your palm i.e. not entering with fingertips first.	Raise your elbow higher.
Your arm straightens when you inhale.	You're straightening your arm to build in extra time to inhale.	Anticipate the turn and inhale quicker, keeping the elbow bent.

  Ex 14J: Flutter kicking and stroking independently

VIDEO   EXERCISE

Learning points:

- Transitioning fully away from the kickboard.

- Getting used to a continual and balanced rocking of the shoulders to power your strokes. One shoulder should be up, whilst the other is down.

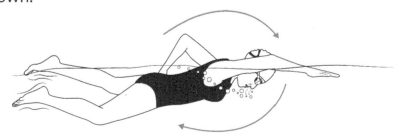

Steps:

1. Inhale above water then exhale slowly and kick with alternating strokes; pulling with your right arm then left arm etc. Remember to *continually* roll the shoulders to power your strokes.

2. Stand up as you get low on air, to inhale.

NOTES

Your head may feel lower in the water. This is a normal reaction to have as you're no longer using the kickboard.

PROBLEM	REASON	SOLUTION
You're swimming zigzag and not straight.	Your hands are entering diagonally, crossing the midline of the body.	Think of entering your left hand at ten o'clock and right hand at two o'clock. Perception can be quite different to reality! You'll most likely be correctly stroking parallel to your body. Repeat Ex 14I holding the kickboard widthways rather than lengthways (as illustrated on the following page*). It'll prompt you to enter the water wider to avoid tapping the kickboard.
You have a stilted/static stroke.	You're thinking of each arm separately rather than as a continuous pull underwater.	Revisit Ex 14I to get used to a smooth stroke without touching the board. **PULLBUOY** Use a pullbuoy to propel yourself only with your arms. Focus on *smooth* strokes rather than *fast* ones. **SNORKEL** You can also wear a snorkel to focus on this. Try starting with one arm up (above your head) and one arm down (by your side).
You're feeling wobbly.	Your head is rolling from side to side as you stroke.	Focus on only rolling shoulders and keeping your head still and centred.
	Your hips are rocking too much.	Keep your hips parallel to the pool floor in order to provide anchoring for your hips and legs.
Your strokes are very rushed.	You're not used to lifting your arms out of the water without an aid.	Imagine trying to inhale with one of your strokes: would you have enough time? If not, slow down your overall stroke speed.

*Holding the kickboard widthways rather than lengthways (to correct a diagonal stroke and avoid swimming zigzag)

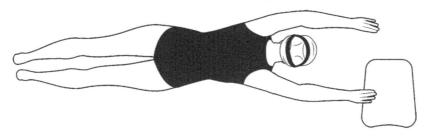

Easier alternatives:

- Practise this exercise with a snorkel.

- If you struggle to move arms and legs together at the same time on your front, practise competitive backstroke (if you've already mastered this). It will build your confidence in multi-tasking the movement of all four limbs simultaneously with a flutter kick and circular arm stroke.

- 'Doggy paddle', flutter kicking and paddling underwater with your head above water.

  Ex 14K: Complete freestyle

VIDEO   EXERCISE

Learning point:

- Incorporating side breathing in order to complete your freestyle.

Steps:

1. Repeat Ex 14J, but rotate head as well as shoulder to inhale as you pull. Inhale on the second, third or fourth stroke (depending on which breathing pattern you've chosen).

TIPS

- *Anticipate the turn and inhalation.*
- *The pull of your opposite arm will help you to roll on your side to inhale e.g. if inhaling towards the right, your left arm will help you to roll towards the right.*
- *Break it down to focus on completing one set of strokes per breath, rather than trying to swim a whole lap of freestyle, which may seem daunting.*
- *If you're able to start linking a set of strokes per breath together, then start counting the number of side breaths you're able to take, rather than the distance you're swimming.*

PROBLEM	REASON	SOLUTION
Your legs are sinking.	You're over dependent on your strokes and have lost focus on the kick.	Start with only the flutter kick (to familiarise yourself with the power) then add in the strokes and breathing.
You're confused about when to breathe.	You've not yet found the rhythm.	Keep counting your strokes until it becomes more automated.
	You may have started to swim with a different arm than usual! People generally always start with the same arm every time.	Practise with the same arm always stroking first, until you have the confidence to change.
	You're rolling your head side to side when exhaling, leading to confusion on when you should be turning for air.	Keep your head centred when face down exhaling and only turn it to the side to inhale.
You're not ready to breathe on the third stroke.	You've not yet found the rhythm.	Instead of counting *up* to the third stroke, try counting *down*; you may exhale faster that way.
You're forgetting to inhale.	This is common! You're still finding your rhythm.	Ensure you exhale so that you *need* to inhale. *Anticipate* the turn and inhalation.
You're not getting enough air or you're getting breathless.	You're not yet confident enough to inhale properly or are lacking stamina to swim for long.	Try to recover your breath in the next turn rather than stopping completely. Stroke faster/inhale deeper/exhale slower. When you inhale, flip onto your back and continue flutter kicking (arms by sides) to catch your breath. Then flip back onto your front to resume freestyling when ready.

PROBLEM	REASON	SOLUTION
You struggle to inhale on one particular side.	This is common. If you're right-handed, you may find turning to the right more difficult, as your (non-dominant) left arm is supporting you with the turn.	Practise turning to your weaker side only, inhaling every two or four strokes. The repetition will help you to improve and build confidence. (Only try this if you don't anticipate getting confused!)
You're not able to clear the water to inhale/you're catching water.	Your stroke and breath are not in sync.	Focus on pulling with the *opposite* arm of the side you're breathing towards, in order to inhale. Pull and breathe *together*.
	You're not rotating your upper body enough to clear the water.	Take a deep breath and practice exhaling continuously *throughout*; both whilst face down and whilst your head is turned to the side. Focus on gaining consistency in clearing the water level by rolling shoulders and head with every turn. This will give you the confidence to start to inhale with every turn.
You're unsure of the correct speed for the stroke.	This is common and will ultimately depend on your buoyancy as well as how far you plan to swim.	There's a fine line between relaxed strokes (so you don't get worn out) vs enough momentum (to prevent you from sinking). Experiment to work out the right speed for you.

Easier alternative:

- Practise this exercise with a noodle across your hips.

- Practise this exercise with short blade fins.

15: ADVANCED SKILLS

15.1 Linking laps between strokes

Ex 15A: Front torpedo ('push and glide')
Ex 15B: Back torpedo ('push and glide')
Ex 15C: From a front stroke to a front stroke: touch turn
Ex 15D: From a front stroke to a back stroke: turn
Ex 15E: From a back stroke to a front stroke: turn
Ex 15F: From a back stroke to a back stroke: turn

15.2 Linking between treading water and a stroke

Ex 15G: From treading water to a front stroke
Ex 15H: From treading water to a back stroke
Ex 15I: From a front or back stroke to treading water

15.3 Confidence in deep water

Ex 15J: Resurfacing after submerging into deep water
Ex 15K: Snorkelling
Ex 15L: Swimming over deep water
Ex 15M: Swimming underwater

15.4 Swimming in open water

ALERT

Your safety is the highest priority. To undertake exercises in this chapter you must already be able to swim a stroke and tread water. Be truthful with yourself about your own capabilities. A student Nadia assured me that she could already tread water but wasn't honest with either herself or me! (It meant I had to rescue her when she panicked in the deep end.)

Swimming towards or over deep water may make your heart race – it does with many of my students. If you feel too anxious or nervous by yourself, then take a buddy with you who is calm, patient, supportive and a good swimmer.

15.1 LINKING LAPS BETWEEN STROKES

VIDEO   EXERCISE   **Ex 15A: Front torpedo ('push and glide')**

Steps:

1. Stand with your back facing the wall and one foot raised flat against the wall.

2. Place your dominant hand flat on top of your non-dominant hand and wrap your dominant thumb around your non-dominant hand. This locks your hands into place (as illustrated below).

   Hand position for torpedo (if right-handed)

3. Extend your arms straight above your head and close to your ears.

4. Inhale and bend forward to exhale face down.

5. Place your second foot next to your first foot flat against the wall.

6. Push off with both feet, face down. Arms and legs should be straight and together in a streamlined position. Head remains still and centred.

7. Glide for as long as you can (with one slow exhalation), before standing to inhale.

NOTES

- *You can push off with one foot rather than two, however it's possible that you might launch at a tangent and not glide in a straight line.*
- *You'll know when the glide is coming to an end as you'll start to get wobbly. This is a sign that you're losing momentum.*

TIPS

It's normal to find it more difficult to launch in deep water, so practise launching in shallow water first.

Easier alternative:

- Practise this exercise with a kickboard; holding it with arms outstretched (as illustrated below).

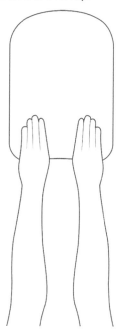

VIDEO   EXERCISE

Ex 15B: Back torpedo ('push and glide')

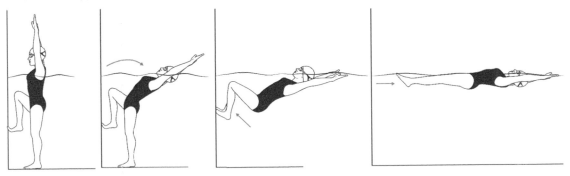

Steps:

1. Stand facing the wall and one foot touching the wall.

2. Place your dominant hand on top of your non-dominant hand and wrap your dominant thumb around your non-dominant hand. This locks your hands into place.

Hand position for torpedo (if right-handed)

3. Extend your arms straight above your head and close to your ears.

4. Inhale and lean backwards whilst exhaling (this is in case you submerge, so you can block the water from entering your mouth and nose).

5. Place your second foot next to your first foot flat against the wall.

6. Continue to exhale as you launch (this is in case you submerge, so you can block the water from entering your mouth and nose). Push off with both feet, face up. Arms and legs should be straight and together in a streamlined position. Head remains still and centred.

7. As your glide loses momentum, stand up.

NOTES

- *You can push off with one foot rather than two, however it's possible that you might launch at a tangent and not glide in a straight line.*
- *You'll know when the glide is coming to an end as you'll start to get wobbly. This is a sign that you're losing momentum.*

TIPS

- *It's normal to find it more difficult to launch in deep water, so practise launching in shallow water first.*

Easier alternative:

- Practise this exercise with a kickboard, holding it against your chest (as illustrated below).

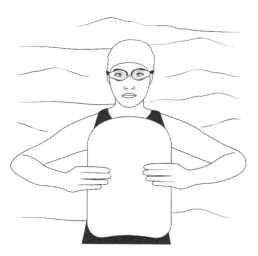

VIDEO

EXERCISE

Ex 15C: From a front stroke to a front stroke: touch turn

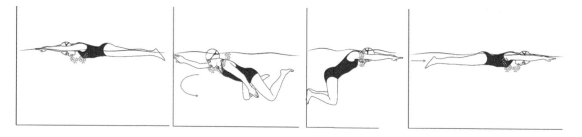

1. Consider which way you wish to turn when approaching the wall, and then leave your *opposite* hand on the wall to pivot your body around.

   For example, if you choose to turn towards the left, use your right hand to pivot your body around.

2. Once you've turned around with your back facing the wall, launch with a front torpedo. Push off with both feet, face down. Arms and legs should be straight and together in a streamlined position. Head remains still and centred.

3. As your glide loses momentum, start swimming again.

Try not to break your stroke pattern. That's to say, you can do the turn with either head down or up, depending on where you are in the stroke with the breathing as you approach the wall.

TIPS

PROBLEM	REASON	SOLUTION
You're too far from the wall to be able to push off after turning.	You're anticipating the turn too soon.	Practise. The timing to start the turn will be based on the speed that you're swimming. Your body must be close enough to the wall for your hand then feet to touch it.
You get stuck during the turn and can't push off.	You're slowing down before reaching the wall.	Keep the same pace otherwise you'll lose momentum and not be able to launch.
You're rushing as you approach the wall in order to perform the turn with head up.	You're worried about where you are in your breathing with the stroke when doing the turn.	Focus on ensuring you don't break your rhythm e.g. if you're exhaling face down, continue the turn with head down.
You're not able to glide well.	You're rushing the turn.	Practise slower. Practise with a snorkel to slow down. SNORKEL
	Your legs aren't streamlined.	Launch from the wall with legs straight and together.
You're gliding at a tangent.	You pushed off the wall with only one foot.	Push off the wall with both feet together.
Your feet keep touching the bottom during the turn.	You're doing the turn too slowly, causing your legs to drop.	Try in slightly deeper water where it's easier to turn slower without standing. Practise with a snorkel. When your head is down; it'll be easier to keep your feet up. SNORKEL

NOTES

A touch turn is a much simpler way to link laps compared with a tumble turn (that's performed in competitive swimming). It's of particular benefit if you suffer from motion sickness because it doesn't involve doing a somersault in the water.

Technically speaking touch turns are meant to link only breaststroke laps, however there's no reason why you can't use it with freestyle too.

It's useful if you can practice turning in both directions, for situations where the pool dictates a certain direction of swimming laps (either clockwise or anti-clockwise), as illustrated in Chapter 6 'Getting ready: practicalities'.

Easier alternative:

- Practise this exercise widthways if your pool allows it; launching with a front torpedo and then doing the touch turn as you approach the wall.

VIDEO   EXERCISE

Ex 15D: From a front stroke to a back stroke: turn

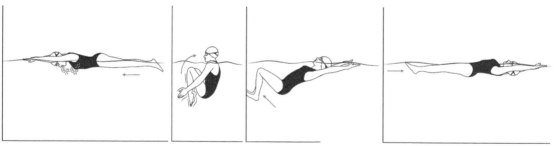

Steps:

1. As you approach the wall on your front, curl up into a ball and launch with a back torpedo. Push off with both feet, face up. Arms and legs should be straight and together in a streamlined position. Head remains still and centred.

2. As your glide loses momentum, start swimming again.

TIPS

Remember to exhale as you launch (this is in case you submerge, so you can block the water from entering your mouth and nose).

NOTES *This exercise is particularly useful if you get tired or breathless with swimming on your front. Swimming a recovery lap on your back can help to catch your breath again.*

Easier alternative:

- Practise this exercise by launching with arms by your sides rather than above your head.

 VIDEO EXERCISE **Ex 15E: From a back stroke to a front stroke: turn**

Steps:

1. As you approach the wall on your back, extend one arm above your head so you can touch the wall with your hand.

2. Inhale and roll forward to curl into a ball whilst exhaling.

3. Launch with a front torpedo. Push off with both feet, face down. Arms and legs should be straight and together in a streamlined position. Head remains still and centred.

4. As your glide loses momentum, start swimming again.

Ex 15F: From a back stroke to a back stroke: turn

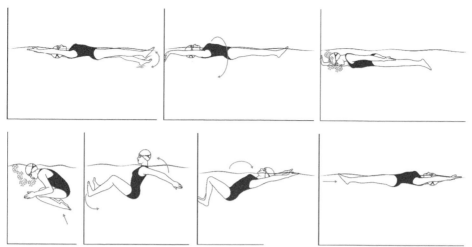

Steps:

1. As you approach the wall on your back, extend one arm above your head so you can touch the wall with your hand.

2. Inhale then exhale whilst flipping onto your front so you're now facing the wall.

3. Curl up into a ball and launch with a back torpedo. Push off with both feet, face up. Arms and legs should be straight and together in a streamlined position. Head remains still and centred.

4. As your glide loses momentum, start swimming again.

15.2 LINKING BETWEEN TREADING WATER AND A STROKE

Ex 15G: From treading water to a front stroke

Steps:

1. Tread water.

2. Inhale, lean forwards and exhale face down.

3. Kick and paddle until you're horizontal.

4. Front float.

5. Bring your arms and legs together in a streamlined position then start swimming.

TIPS

- *As you get more proficient, you can skip step 4.*

EXERCISE **Ex 15H: From treading water to a back stroke**

Steps:

1. Tread water.

2. Inhale, lean backwards and exhale (this is in case you submerge, so you can block the water from entering your mouth and nose).

3. Kick and paddle until you're horizontal.

4. Back float.

5. Bring your arms and legs together in a streamlined position then start swimming.

TIPS

- *As you get more proficient, you can skip step 4.*

EXERCISE **Ex 15I: From a front or back stroke to treading water**

- When swimming on your back, kick and paddle to lean *forwards* until your body is upright. Start treading as soon as your body is vertical.

- When swimming on your front, kick and paddle to lean *backwards* until your body is upright (exhaling until your face is clear of the water). Start treading as soon as your body is vertical.

TIPS

- *Don't wait to start treading water!*

15.3 CONFIDENCE IN DEEP WATER

 Ex 15J: Resurfacing after submerging into deep water

 • *To jump (or dive) into water, the minimum safe depth required is the total height of yourself with your arm outstretched above your head, i.e. at least one and a half times your height.*

Steps:

1. Stand at the pool side and inhale.

2. Start exhaling as you jump into the water feet first.

3. Kick and paddle until you resurface. (It doesn't matter which kick you do.)

4. Once your mouth is above water, you can either tread, float or swim.

 • *Ration out your bubbles (i.e. exhale slowly) to allow time to resurface without panicking that you're losing air too quickly.*

Easier alternatives (to gain confidence before attempting the above exercise):

• Start at a depth where you can stand on your tip-toes. Inhale, bend your knees to raise your feet from the pool floor and exhale as you submerge. Practise the above exercise from step 3 onwards.

• Sit on the pool side with legs submerged. Inhale then exhale as you roll forwards into the water, and practise the above exercise from step 3 onwards. It'll be safer to try this in shoulder depth if you're not confident about resurfacing. (Rolling forward into the water won't cause you to somersault.)

  Ex 15K: Snorkelling

 • *For this section you must already be familiar with using a snorkel and wearing fins.*

NOTES *Snorkelling fins have longer blades compared with short blade swim training fins. This helps to conserve energy when observing marine life as you need to kick much less in order to propel yourself forward.*

- **To move slowly:** flutter kick with either your arms by your sides or arms behind your back.

- **To move faster:** flutter kick with either breaststroke arm stroke or freestyle arm stroke.

- **To stay in one spot:** flutter kick with sculls Y stronger than sculls X (refer to Ex 11B).

 EXERCISE ## Ex 15L: Swimming over deep water

Five steps (explained below) to build confidence in swimming over deep water

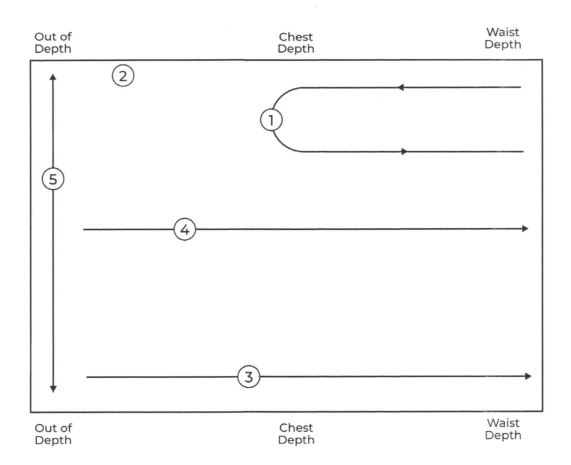

1. Swim where you can stand and get used to changing direction without touching the pool floor or the pool edge. You could incorporate some treading water when changing direction if you wish. This will give you the confidence to then try this out of depth. In theory if you can do this where you can stand, you can also do it where you can't.

2. Guide yourself along the pool edge with your hands and familiarise yourself out of depth by bobbing up and down facing the pool edge, bouncing off the bottom with your toes. Remember to exhale when submerged. Feel the 'upthrust' of the water pushing you up towards the surface. Do this first whilst holding the pool edge with your hands at all times, and then see if you can repeat the exercise while letting go during your submersion, perhaps with one hand first, before trying with both.

3. Swim lengthways from deep to shallow water, staying close to the pool edge in case you panic. This will get you familiar with starting to swim from where you can't stand. It's also easier psychologically to swim from deep to shallow rather than vice versa.

4. Repeat step 3 away from arm's reach of the pool edge.

5. Swim widthways (if your pool allows) across the deep water staying close to the pool edge in case you panic. This is ideal if you have a narrow pool, as you can try swimming a short distance over deep water.

NOTES

- *Deep water is defined as a depth where if you stand with your feet flat on the ground, the water level covers your mouth.*
- *If you have a pre-existing 'familiar' stroke (which you learnt when younger), it's likely that you'll default to swimming this if you panic in deep water as your survival instinct kicks in. I've seen this plenty of times before, for example where a student is learning freestyle and reverts to breaststroke when out of depth.*

Ex 15M: Swimming underwater

VIDEO   EXERCISE

Steps:

1. Inhale.

2. Exhale face down and use your breaststroke arms with a flutter kick.

TIPS

- *Make sure your head is pointing in the direction of travel i.e. downward.*
- *Pull your arms and kick hard in order to dive down; this is because the water will be pushing your body upwards towards the surface.*
- *Make sure you ration out your bubbles (i.e. exhale slowly) to allow time to resurface without panicking that you're losing air too quickly.*
- *Don't curl up into a ball, as this will result in you floating.*

15.4 SWIMMING IN OPEN WATER

This is very different to swimming in the controlled environment of a swimming pool. It can be a fun and exhilarating experience, but you'll need to be a confident and reasonably fit swimmer, who can also tread water because depths can vary considerably and won't be signposted of course.

Considerations:

- Check if the waterway is patrolled. If it isn't and you still wish to swim, take a buddy with you.

- Check depths (if possible). If there are other people in the water, are they able to stand?

- Check tidal conditions.

- Check for hidden hazards. For example are there any hidden rocks, drops in the sandbanks, algae on rocks that would make them slippery?

- Check rip conditions.

- Check wave conditions. You may need to swim underwater (refer to Ex 15M) if you wish to duck under the waves and swim in calmer water.

Pros and cons of the three mainstream strokes in open water:

- **Backstroke** (either competitive or survival)

  It can be difficult to understand where you are as you'll undoubtedly only see sky! It can be more practical to swim on your front in open water, as you're able to do what's called 'sighting' where you can regularly track your position against a fixed object whilst swimming parallel to the coastline. Backstroke is however a very useful way to be able to swim if you get tired/breathless in open water, particularly survival backstroke.

- **Breaststroke** (either competitive or survival)

  It gives you the best peripheral frontal vision of your direction of travel and your surrounds, particularly survival breaststroke.

- **Freestyle**

  It's strongly recommended to be able to breathe on either side (i.e. bilaterally). This is because you can do 'sighting' (explained above) regardless of your swimming direction and adapt to external environmental factors (e.g. waves in your face or the sun's position in your eyes).

FINAL THOUGHTS

Thank you for using this book. I hope you found it beneficial to get more confident in the water, whatever your goals are.

I'd really appreciate your review on Amazon – it would help to inspire and encourage more adults to take the plunge!

Contact details

If you have any questions or feedback, please feel free to get in touch:

Email: petrina@swimwithasmile.com

Website: www.swimwithasmile.com

Facebook: www.facebook.com/swimwithasmile

Instagram: www.instagram.com/swimwithasmile

Useful links

AUSTSWIM: Australia's national organisation for the Teaching of Swimming and Water Safety™
www.austswim.com.au

Royal Life Saving Society Australia: a water safety, swimming and lifesaving education organisation
www.royallifesaving.com.au

Surf Life Saving Australia: a not-for-profit community organisation that promotes water safety and provides surf rescue services
www.sls.com.au and www.beachsafe.org.au

Speedo®: a brand that sells swim equipment and swimwear
www.speedo.com.au

Zoggs®: a brand that sells swim equipment and swimwear
www.zoggs.com.au

Happy swimming!

GLOSSARY

I've used layman's terms throughout this book wherever possible to avoid getting too technical. There are however a few words that may prove helpful to explain here as a point of reference.

- **Arm stroke:** a way to move your arms in the water.
- **Backstroke (competitive):** a way to swim on your back (face up) with arms moving in a backward circular motion above and below the water together with legs flutter kicking.
- **Backstroke (survival):** a way to swim on your back (face up) with forearms moving close to the body in the water together with legs whip kicking.
- **Back torpedo:** otherwise known as a 'push and glide'. A launch of the body in a streamlined position, horizontally with face up.
- **Bilateral breathing:** the skill in freestyle of alternating breathing on each side i.e. turning to inhale every third or fifth stroke. Inhaling every third stroke is technically the correct way.
- **Breaststroke (competitive):** a way to swim on your front (face down) with arms moving in a sweeping motion below the water alternately to legs whip kicking.
- **Breaststroke (survival):** a way to swim on your front (face up) with whole arms moving in a sweeping motion below the water alternately to legs whip kicking.
- **Buoyancy:** the force of water pushing your body upwards (as illustrated below).
- **Catching water:** this is my own term to describe getting water in the mouth or nose.
- **Doggy paddle:** a way to swim on your front (head up) with arms paddling underwater together with legs flutter kicking. A term used to reflect the same way that dogs swim.
- **Drag:** a synonym for resistance i.e. hindrance on motion through water. It's referenced in this book in two contexts: loose fitting clothing and incorrect body positioning.

- **Drowning:** respiratory impairment from submersion-immersion in liquid[6]. There are three possible outcomes: survival without any detrimental effects, survival with severe/persisting injuries, or death.

- **Flex foot/ankle:** curl your toes towards your knees. It's referenced in this book as an important part of the whip kick.

- **Float:** a skill to stay at the water's surface (without sinking) either in a horizontal or vertical body position.

- **Flutter kick:** movement of the legs up and down in a streamlined position and in an alternating continuous action from your hips. Your knees should bend slightly with loose ankles and floppy feet.

- **Freestyle/front crawl:** technically it can mean any stroke, but usually refers to a way to swim on your front (face down) with arms moving in a forward circular motion above and below the water together with legs flutter kicking.

- **Front torpedo:** otherwise known as a 'push and glide'. A launch of the body in a streamlined position, horizontally with face down.

- **Glide:** a movement through water in a streamlined position with arms or legs motionless. It's referenced in this book in terms of a component of breaststroke and torpedoes.

- **Gravity:** the force of the Earth pulling your body downwards (see illustration below).

- **Kick:** a way to move your legs in the water.

- **Open water:** a body of water which is not enclosed e.g. the ocean.

- **Propulsion:** the force that moves your body in the desired direction (see illustration below).

- **Resistance:** the force of water pushing against the desired direction. 'Frontal resistance' is the force of water pushing against the front of a swimmer (frontal resistance can be generated by a slightly raised head as illustrated below).

- **Rip:** a strong, steady current of water that flows out from the shore in the direction that causes least resistance.

- **Sculling:** a movement of the hands in an outwards and inwards sweeping motion underwater, with fingers close together. It's referenced in this book twice: for treading water and and as a way to swim on your back.

- **Set:** completing a certain distance (based on your ability) of an exercise. I deliberately use the word 'set' rather than 'lap' as 'lap' may be a daunting and/or difficult task to complete.
- **Sighting:** a skill to regularly track your location in the water against a fixed object. Usually referenced in open water swimming parallel to the coastline.
- **Streamlined position:** arms and/or legs are straight and together in order to maximise the efficiency of movement through water and minimise resistance.
- **Stroke:** a way to move your whole body in order to get from A to B in water.
- **Treading water:** a technique to survive in deep water by maintaining an upright position with mouth above the water level in order to breathe easily.
- **Unilateral breathing:** the skill in freestyle of breathing on just one side i.e. turning to inhale every second or fourth stroke.
- **Whip kick:** movement of the legs by bringing heels towards your bottom and kicking with flexed feet outwards in a circular motion before snapping legs back together. Otherwise known as the frog kick.

The four forces on the body in water

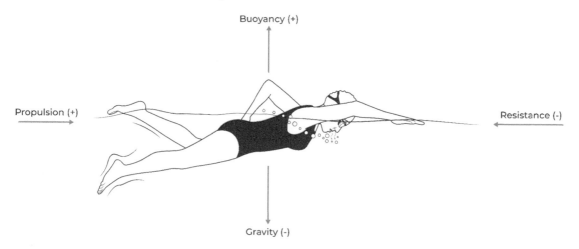

Buoyancy (+)

Propulsion (+)

Resistance (-)

Gravity (-)

REFERENCES

1. Royal Life Saving National Drowning Report 2019, Sydney Australia

2. Royal Life Saving National Drowning Report 2019, Sydney Australia

3. 'Swimming and All-Cause Mortality Risk Compared With Running, Walking, and Sedentary Habits in Men' paper by Nancy L. Chase, Xuemei Sui, and Steven N. Blair (2008)

4. The Complete Guide to Aqua Exercise for Pregnancy and Postnatal Health by Sarah Bolitho & Vicky Hatch (2014)

5. Make the Pool Your Gym: No-Impact Water Workouts for Getting Fit, Building Strength and Rehabbing from Injury by Karl Knopf (2012)

6. Swimming & Lifesaving: Water Safety for all Australians by Royal Life Saving Australia (2010)

INDEX

Printed at Repro India Ltd.